Taking Your Life Back

Rick Shelton

D1472254

Unless otherwise indicated, all Scripture quotations are taken from the *New King James Version* ®. Copyright © 1982 by Thomas Nelson, Inc. Used by permission. All rights reserved.

Scripture quotations marked AMP are taken from the *Amplified® Bible*, Copyright © 1954, 1958, 1962, 1964, 1965, 1987 by The Lockman Foundation. Used by permission. (www.Lockman.org)

Scripture quotations marked KJV are taken from the *King James Version* of the Bible.

Scripture quotations marked NIV are taken from THE HOLY BIBLE, NEW INTERNATIONAL VERSION®, NIV® Copyright © 1973, 1978, 1984, 2011 by Biblica, Inc.® Used by permission. All rights reserved worldwide.

Foreword

by Joyce Meyer

Rick Shelton has been my friend for over thirty years. When we met, he was twenty-six and I was thirty-six. He had just begun a church, and I was the second employee he hired for his new staff. Within the next couple of years, I began a women's ministry there. Rick and Donna gave me some of my first opportunities in ministry, and I will always love and appreciate them for it. They both have a deep desire to serve God and help people.

I was excited to read the early manuscript of "Taking Your Life Back." In this book, Rick shares how his desire to serve God and help people drove him to the point of physical, mental and emotional exhaustion. Like many of us who are strong-willed, driven individuals, he pushed himself beyond reasonable limits and broke every biblical guideline that God has given us concerning rest and balance. His motive was right, but his method was wrong. I understand this area all too well. I too had to learn this lesson the hard way.

Rick shares intimate details of his six-year illness that literally became a nightmare, not only for him, but also for his family and many who knew and loved him. His candid approach will be a tremendous blessing to anyone who is battling anxiety, panic attacks, depression, insomnia and other mysterious illnesses that are real, but sometimes difficult to diagnose.

His recovery is nothing less than amazing and it will give every reader hope that they too can overcome. This book is a wonderful testimony to the faithfulness and healing power of God.

I am confident that reading "Taking Your Life Back," will empower you to resist passivity and fear and be the bold and powerful person that God intends you to be. I truly believe the possibilities of a healed life are limitless.

Joyce Meyer

Table of Contents

Preface

We live in stressful times. Fear is at epidemic proportions. Depression is rampant. Yet something inside of you knows you were created for a life of *meaning* and *purpose*. You are pre-programmed with *destiny*…born to conquer and designed for *success*. Early in life, you sensed inwardly that you had the potential for becoming something grand. But in every life, many of those hopes and dreams are shattered as difficulties and painful situations coming one after another converge to destroy your hope of ever fulfilling all you know you could be.

With that being the case, there are questions you should ask yourself in order to recognize the effects these difficulties are creating in your life. They have the capability of causing even greater harm than all of the painful situations you have endured. Do you have trouble sleeping? Are you depressed? Are you suffering from panic attacks or anxiety? Are you physically ill or mentally tormented? Are you a workaholic living on the edge of burn out? Do you feel like you are trapped in a maze, always running but never making progress?

This book is the story of the crisis that I (and my family) endured…from how it all began, all the way through the battles, heartaches, tears and conquests, to my present day life of healing, freedom, restored peace and vision for the future. I have related my own time-tested principles and practical guidelines for health and well-being from a strictly personal experiential point of view.

Though this book is designed to provide accurate and helpful information, we are making it available with the understanding that we are not providing specific medical or psychological advice or other professional services. If you need medical or psychological advice, we encourage you to seek out the services of competent professionals in the area of your need. If you need real answers from a practical point of view, this book is for you.

How to Get the Most Out of This Book:

- The first half of this book is the story of everything I went through—from how it began, all the way through the fight to its successful conclusion, and to the present.

- I have listed some telltale danger signs to be aware of.

- Use this book as a mirror. What do you identify with?

- The second part of this book contains vital truths to study and learn, regardless of the battle you are facing.

- There are also practical guidelines for health and well-being given from a strictly experiential point of view.

Practical Study Suggestions:

- Get a notebook and pen. As you read, make little notes to yourself about anything that applies to you.

- Have a highlighter handy at all times. This will help you refer back to important statements you want to remember.

- Have your Bible close by. Scriptures are not quoted word for word, allowing the reader to stay in the flow of what is being said. The scripture references are listed for you to easily study later.

- Go to a comfortable and quiet place without distractions. It is easier for your heart to be spoken to as well as your mind in that kind of setting.

Endorsements

Throughout history nations have fought against nations and the victory would come to the army that would capture the capital city, flag, or general of the opposing nation. That is the same method Satan has uses to destroy the Church. He attempts to destroy the ministers that God has called to be His generals.

In his book, "Taking Your Life Back," Pastor Rick Shelton takes you on a journey that shows how the forces of darkness plot to destroy God's children. But the story doesn't stop there. Pastor Rick also shows how you can walk through the enemy's camp and not only survive, but become victorious over the enemy.

Pastor Rick shows through his statement, "The only avenue to your authority is through your will," that while surrendering your will to the Lord may sound like the religious thing to do, God is looking for submission, not surrender. God has actually given us self-control (Galatians 5:23) and authority while empowering us with His grace to overcome even the darkest times.

Although Pastor Rick takes you through the perils of tragedy, he then reveals the path to victory. For those dealing with discouragement or even burnout, this book is a must read.

This book will be a blessing to everyone who is walking through the fire and trials of life and will be encouraged by Pastor Rick and Donna Shelton's testimony of victory. If you apply the principles in "Taking Your Life Back" you will move from the depths of depression & pain into a place of victory and rest.

This book will cause you to leap to your feet and know that not only is victory possible, but that it can be attained.

Dr. Larry Ollison, Pastor of Walk on the Water Faith Church

Within the pages of this book, I found hope. Pastor Rick's humility in sharing the details of his battle through the dark days of panic and anxiety provided me with the direction and encouragement that I had been crying out for. Shining his light through this testimony helped me to see that I didn't have to live the rest of my life in the grip of fear and panic, and that freedom is possible. Many of my relatives have lived with this and I was determined to prove that God alone is sufficient to heal me and set me free without turning to prescription medications. Pastor Rick's book gave me just what I needed to keep on in faith that God would help me to win the victory. Today I am free and I am thankful that such a powerful resource is available to us.

Lupe Castello - wife, stay home mom of 4

Completely captivating, I found it difficult to put this book down. Pastor Shelton's willingness to be courageously transparent about his struggle with life threatening burnout and his healing process is unprecedented. This subject has been kept in the dark far too long. Pastor Shelton brings it into the light with the hope of healing for victims of burnout who are willing to reach for it. For those in the unrelenting deadly grasp of burnout, in any phase, this book could very well save your ministry, work and possibly your life.

Patrick Bradley, Founder and President, International Crisis Aid

I sat down to read the table of contents and thought I would read chapter 1 to get the gist of it. Within the next hour or so I wept myself to the end!

Riveting, real and revelational with the power to revolutionize...it carries the quality of Spirit-birthed empathy to minister hope that will help others...surely this is what the Apostle Paul meant by 2nd Cor.1:4...

Dr. Eddy Brown,

President, International College of Bible Theology

Introduction

This is a tell-all...

I only wish someone had put a book like this in my hands during the six years I was going through these difficulties. As it was, I read everything I could get my hands on that I thought would address even a few of my issues. I was desperate to get some understanding about what was happening to me. There were precious few books that shed any real light or helped me understand my situation.

With so many people suffering from adrenal exhaustion, panic attacks, anxiety, and nerve and sleep disorders, I thought surely there would at least be one self-help book that would address one or two of these issues. Though probably written with great intentions, what I found was a lot of books that were "way out there," as far as real life application was concerned. In fact, I found only one book, *The Hidden Link Between Adrenaline and Stress*, by Dr. Archibald Hart, which gave me valuable information about the adrenal issue from a balanced medical and biblical viewpoint. However, as helpful as this book was, I needed information on the other issues I was dealing with as well. I was desperate for someone to help me shut down this internal drive that was running me non-stop.

I was reeling from being hit with many different symptoms all at once as well as difficult situations coming at us one after another. Like a drowning man, I was grasping for any kind of lifeline. If I had discovered even one book, like this one, to show me that someone had gone through and survived what I was experiencing, I would have devoured it from cover to cover. If the author was willing to be painfully transparent, sharing everything—successes and mistakes—I know I would not have needlessly suffered for as long as I did. In fact, I would have locked myself in a room with the book and not have come out until I was completely healed.

Why I am telling my story...

I was sick for over six years…close to death *twice*. Before I was restored back to health, the Lord had to open my eyes so I could see certain things. Once I understood them, it took only twelve days for me to receive my healing. *Twelve days*…after six long, painful, desperate years!

What you don't know can kill you. Truth forgotten is equally as deadly. It is amazing what receiving the right information can do.

Five days after being healed, the Lord totally set me free from an unhealthy dependency on prescription medicines prescribed to control daily panic attacks and to help me sleep. Though I am grateful for medicines that actually improve the quality of people's lives, in my particular case, the medicines were masking the real issues that needed to be addressed. I had been taking them for years, in the highest dosages and maximum strengths. Several times I tried to wean myself off of them, and though I made progress, I could never break completely free in my own strength.

While the doctors were trying to find the right combination of medications for me, much of the time I functioned like a zombie. I was hardly coherent. Obviously, that's not very flattering to tell about myself. Why am I telling these things? Because although the details are embarrassing, I am compelled to share how God has been so good to me in order for you to find hope - even if your situation seems hopelessly desperate.

My attitude before I became sick...

I have always been intrigued by the life of Elijah in the Bible. He was a great man of God, used mightily as a voice in his day. Then, at what seemed to be the peak of his ministry, his boldness turned to cowardice, his strength to weakness, and his confidence melted into anxiety and depression.

I read the account of that season of Elijah's life and for years, did not understand how this great man of God could be reduced to such a pitiful state. He ran away like a fearful coward into the wilderness, crawled under a broom tree and prayed to die (I Kings 19:3). This is the same man who had called down rain to break a terrible drought and outran a chariot *on foot* to get to shelter before the torrent began...incredible!

Elijah had just single-handedly faced down the prophets of Baal and dealt them a crushing defeat by calling down fire from

God to destroy their altars and burn up their water-soaked sacrifice. Yet, when the wife of the king threatened to have him killed, Elijah immediately ran for his life like a whipped pup. This, I could not understand. What suddenly happened to all his strength, power, and courage?

I thought to myself, *I would never behave the way Elijah did after such a great success for God.* It was unthinkable to me that I would let a single threat from one person send me into a tailspin of panic and fear that would cause me to despair of life itself. *That would never happen to me. I would handle the situation correctly,* I thought.

I judged Elijah's weakness, as we all are prone to do when we stand apart from something we have never personally experienced. How wrong I was. Nothing I had ever heard or read about prepared me for what I was about to experience.

I was relatively young…still in my 40's…my power years. Up until this time, I had never suffered any major physical, mental or emotional blows in my personal life that were overwhelming or life-threatening.

Having started LIFECHURCH with only nineteen people in a hotel room in 1980, I thought I had experienced most of the bumps in the road that could come from pioneering a growing church from that humble beginning to a thriving congregation. LIFECHURCH quickly became an incubator for varying types of ministries and missionaries to be developed and launched around the world.

God had graced me with a message and an anointing that

connected with the hearts of people. As a result, I was given opportunities to travel extensively to many nations of the world. I must say, though, I mistakenly thought that the strength I ministered in would cover me outside the pulpit as well. In other words, I thought that I could get by with ignoring the persisting symptoms and weakness in my body. This wrong thinking was costly and nearly deadly.

Soon, I would enter into the darkest, most painful period of my entire life…

For six very long years, I experienced a downward spiral that touched every area of my life—physical, mental, emotional and relational. For the first time since I entered the ministry, I began to lose my confidence and seriously questioned my ability to lead. I took every criticism directed at me as truth, because I no longer had the strength or courage to withstand it. At first, I thought, *Surely this will be over shortly.* Later I thought, *This cannot possibly last much longer or get any worse.* But in both instances, I was wrong. I became a person I didn't even recognize—a cowering, fearful, shadow of the strong, faith-filled man I had once been.

But God…

Just like with Elijah, God came on the scene, put His finger on the problem, provided the *answer* and set me on the path of miraculous healing and physical restoration. Since that day, I have told my story to friends. I have shared my journey to recovery with people in many churches and conferences around the world. People have sobbed on my shoulder, sent emails, and asked for prayer. They are so thankful to find someone who has experienced the horror they are now going through, and who is willing to tell all.

I never realized how many people are in despair, fearful they will not make it out of this dark time to live normally again. There is an agony, a deep sorrowful pain…a quiet desperation that I know so well and recognize in others that is impossible to explain to someone who has never experienced such things.

Words fail to adequately convey the feelings of complete isolation and "apartness" that one experiences when going through these difficulties. It is like being in a room together with those you love, yet segregated by an invisible barrier, having no way to reach the object of your affection. At the same time, they do not understand your distance or your anguish.

It is a cruel irony that in desperately trying to be "normal," the real issue that ignited the whole problem gets pushed into the background and becomes nearly impossible to bring out of its hiding place. That is why I am telling my story—the good, the bad and the ugly—to show you a path already beaten out through my pain and tears, for you to follow to healing and restoration. God wants to help you find the keys that will unlock your situation. It is my prayer that my story will encourage and inspire you.

There is hope....

I learned my lesson the hard way. Out of all I have been through, I have come to understand that God really wants to use me, but not to the extent that I violate the physical laws He has established for my good. He wants me for the marathon, not just the sprint.

It is somewhat difficult to be this open about my mistakes, yet on the other hand, I know that if even one person avoids the terrible pit I fell into, it is worth any embarrassment I may experience by sharing all of the gory details. Writing this book is my way of sharing with you on a very personal level, with the hope that wherever you are as you read this, you will know - there is help. Regardless of the setbacks, the effects on your family, the severity of your discouragement or your present circumstances, now is the time for you to begin Taking Your Life Back.

Rick Shelton

Chapter One

Hindsight is 20/20

I t would be wonderful if we knew ahead of time all the lessons we would learn while going through a trial. If we could glimpse into the future to see how others would be helped from the wisdom we gleaned in the fire of our crisis, the overwhelming circumstances of the present wouldn't seem so intimidating to us. We would take great courage regardless of the mountains we face.

We are instructed to walk by faith and not by sight (2 Corinthians 5:7), because after our trial is over, we can look back and clearly see what we could not see at the time—the mighty hand of a faithful God clearly guiding us. I can truly say that my life has been completely and dramatically changed by the trials I have gone through. I am profoundly grateful for every discovery and every victory. With fresh revelation of God's Word, I have come to know God's love and peace with a depth I had never known before.

Anyone who has fought against incredible hardship or stared in the face of death will tell you, "Never take one day or one moment for granted!" Once you face something like this, you will begin to see each and every moment as an incredible gift from God. You will also learn that much of what you once thought was so important doesn't really matter in the whole scheme of things. Coming that close to eternity gives a person a proper perspective of their present circumstances. These extreme situations begin to lose their ability to intimidate you and seem less formidable once you realize that, one way or another, God will not abandon you. I have learned to look for beauty in the chaos...light in the darkness.

Perhaps my greatest discovery on my journey to healing was a truth I had known, but allowed to slip. Simply put, God has done His part. He will not do ours. He will not violate the authority He has given us to take charge of and rule over our own bodies and lives. He provided guidelines. It is up to us to follow them. This is an essential truth, and this is where the story of taking my life back begins.

I never wanted to be a preacher in the first place. I told God I would serve Him and help in church, but being a preacher wasn't on my agenda. As a young man with a beautiful wife, Donna, my first son, Jeff, and a good job, my focus was on success and supporting my family. Second to all of that, I was an active member of a church and was happy to help God on the weekends.

I had been pretty content with my life up to that point, but I slowly began to grow discontented, even miserable. This misery culminated in me quitting my job. I vividly remember throwing myself across my bed, crying out to God. He showed me a blank sheet of paper and asked me to sign it. I promised that of course I would, if He would write something on it *first*.

His reply was, "First, *you* sign the paper, and then I will begin to write *My* will for your life on it." I signed the paper and the first thing He wrote was "Preach my Gospel!" Instantly, my "no desire to preach" changed to a driving passion to teach His Word, pastor and help leaders. In June, 1980, we began Life Christian Church in a tiny meeting room with only 19 people at the Viking Lodge in Sunset Hills, Missouri.

We watched God bless our tiny beginning. During this time, I was invited to speak many places in the United States as well as abroad. I knew God had called me to be a voice for Him in my city and around the world. As our church grew, ministry opportunities increased and I worked all the time., even on vacation. I would be on the phone for hours with my team, staying plugged in to make sure no situations would arise without my attention. I thought this was being a good pastor.

Even with all the growth our church experienced, I still had a deep longing for the power and presence of God to change people's lives. This had become the abiding prayer of my heart because, even though we were by no means a dead church, it seemed that there was a decline in miracles. The pastors in our city gathered together once a month for five years to fervently pray for God to move in our churches in a greater way than ever before.

In January of 1994, God answered my prayer and touched me powerfully while I was out of town attending a large meeting in which the presence of God was being felt in a very real and tangible way. When I returned home, that divine encounter began a season in our church that we refer to as "revival." During that time, I saw God impact people with healings and miracles like I hadn't seen for many years. Life situations were dramatically turned around. It was a wonderful season.

As a result of how God had impacted our church, I began to receive many invitations from pastors and leaders around the world who were experiencing the same hunger for the wonderful presence of God. I felt it was a privilege and an honor to be asked to share what God had done for our church. This was also something I knew was part of what I was called to do. It was wonderful to feel needed and wanted in many parts of the world, but I didn't realize that now was the time to decide what was really most important for me to be involved in.

This was an amazing time, but the demands of constant travel and a growing church began to take its toll. I realized to an extent what was happening, but chose to ignore it. I didn't want to miss out on all that God was doing. I would think, *I am just being a good pastor and leader.* I gave myself to each new opportunity without limits or boundaries—without any regard to my physical well-being. Sometimes we deceive ourselves into believing that our choices are justified, perhaps even humble, but nothing could be further from the truth. It is a common trap for many leaders to feel as though they are indispensable when they are being used in a powerful way. This can become a source of pride, if not carefully guarded. We are to be good stewards of everything God has given us, including our bodies.

Chapter Two

Paying the Piper

I thought the fatigue from jet lag was due to my busy travel schedule. Frequently after speaking twice on Sunday, I would leave on Monday for an eight to twelve hour flight to some faraway destination. I would preach, teach and pray for hundreds of people over the course of five days and then start the long journey back, in order to be right on cue for the next Sunday services. I rarely took a Sunday off from ministering at my own church.

After several months, this pace began to wear on me. I began to find it increasingly difficult to sleep. On the rare weeks I didn't travel, I noticed it took longer to get over the constant jet lag. But I couldn't stop. After all, God *needed* me!

I tried to keep up with everything—the church, the constant attention associated with pastoring, and the continual invitations from pastors in other countries. In the midst of all of this, I received devastating news regarding my father-in-law. He was diagnosed with cancer. A few days before his surgery, doctors discovered that Donna's mother also had cancer.

The doctors said that her dad would be fine after his surgery, but after her mother's surgery, the family was told that she was terminal and only had months to live. We were in shock. Donna's mother had always been very healthy and never showed any symptoms until a few days before the diagnosis.

Donna began making frequent trips to Virginia to spend as much time as possible with her parents. During this time, she still tried to keep up with all her extensive oversight of our private elementary and high school, as well as her responsibilities in the church. All of this was in addition to all she did as my wife and the mother of our four sons.

About that same time, our oldest son, Jeff, decided to walk away from the truths he had been taught all of his life. He was in college at the time and began a downward spiral away from God. Never in our wildest dreams did we imagine such a thing might happen. This kind of situation brings a deep, constant pain that defies description. With the pain came self-doubt, accusation, shame, and wondering how we had failed as parents.

The sense of betrayal and judgment that came from totally unexpected sources only added to our pain. People would ask, "If you are such great Christians and pastors, why did your son walk away?" Questions like this along with the incessant gossip, which always found its way back to us, added to the intense pressure and stress we were already experiencing as a result of the situation. During this time, we finally realized to a great extent why pastors and leaders often suffer in silence, reluctant to share their pain. After all, the last thing you want to do when you are hurting is to expose yourself to more pain.

People who have no knowledge or expertise in what you are going through often feel it is their duty to speak freely, as if they were an authority. Sadly, leaders all too often find their families, ministries and motives being judged harshly by people who have never walked one mile in their shoes. Because of the judgmental opinions freely expressed about our family, we reacted by becoming more guarded about sharing the depth of our struggles. Holding everything inside only added to the great pressure and stress we were already experiencing.

Stress is an issue everyone faces. In fact, if you are breathing, you will experience stress. Stress, if handled incorrectly, can invade and destroy as menacingly as any known disease. A camouflaged enemy is the most dangerous enemy you will face. Physical battles are challenging, but the battles that target your mind, heart and emotions can be far more elusive to identify and therefore, far more deadly.

I was unaware that there was an impending storm developing—a storm that would require all of my energy and every scripture hidden in my heart to overcome. At the time, I didn't see the whole picture; I only saw the single issues confronting me. I began to live in survival mode, trying to negotiate each crisis. The constant and pressing issues caused me to lose the ability to see my life as a whole. I lost perspective. This is a common, yet costly, mistake.

What you ignore can be fatal. The sleep issues I was experiencing were the first of many clues that screamed for my attention. Sleeplessness was the first strong indicator that I was ignoring

God's laws concerning my physical body. I found it increasingly difficult to sleep. Along the way I had other, even more alarming, physical issues that were clear indicators that I was crossing lines and heading for a real problem. But I still refused to slow down.

For a period of time, I had what I could only describe as a buzzing in my head. My pastoral staff encouraged me to have it checked out. When I finally met with a neurologist, he said I needed to go somewhere and sleep for at least ten days in order to break this stress cycle. My pastoral team encouraged me to do this, so Donna and I went away for twelve days. I didn't think I was really all that tired. The first day I sat and relaxed all day in a partly shaded spot. The next seven days, I slept continuously, waking up only to eat. Sure enough, after ten days, the buzzing in my head ceased. At that point, I wrongly thought, *That's that; now I can get back to business.*

None of the habits of my workaholic lifestyle changed at that time, so it wasn't long before sleep began to elude me again. Instead of stopping to search for the cause of my sleeplessness, I opted for an easier route—treating the symptoms.

The cost of some mistakes is common, yet very destructive. There is, in fact, a shared denominator in many of the heart-rending stories people have related to Donna and me. For some reason, people don't associate their inability to sleep with the beginning of the horror they are now dealing with in their physical bodies and minds. Sleep is as vital to our health and well being as breathing and eating. The symptomatic lack of rest is a vital indicator that there is an underlying problem which must be dealt with.

I began to try to control my symptoms of sleeplessness by taking over-the-counter sleep aids. This isn't bad or wrong on occasion, but ignoring the reasons for continual sleeplessness is a grave mistake. The various medications I tried only helped for a short time and then, when stressful situations would occur or I would have what seemed to be an onslaught of bad news, even the best over-the-counter sleep aids wouldn't help.

Our Creator knows the maintenance required for the optimal performance of our bodies. So let's take a moment to review a few of His irrefutable laws concerning *rest*. These laws are established for our benefit and are worthy of respect. In other words, these laws are not optional.

First of all, God set the example Himself, when He rested on the seventh day after six days of creating. He then blessed the seventh day and commanded that after working for six days, the seventh would be *holy unto Him*, designated especially for rest (see Genesis 2: 2-3). In the book of Exodus, the seventh day is referred to as "the rest of the holy Sabbath unto the Lord" (see Exodus 16:23).

Under the Law, God told Moses to speak to the children of Israel concerning this day of rest. In fact, He spoke strongly about the issue. He indicated clearly that rest is not optional. In fact, those who disobeyed the command to honor this day and worked when they should have been resting were to be put to death (see Exodus 31:12-17).

Why would God speak so adamantly about rest? We can find answers to this question in the New Testament. Jesus referred to His body as a temple (John 2:19-21). Paul stated clearly, "Do you not know that you are the temple of God and that the Spirit of God dwells in you? If anyone defiles the temple of God, God will destroy him. For the temple of God is holy, which temple you are. Let no one deceive himself..." (1 Corinthians 3:16-18). If we take scripture seriously, Christians should be the most healthy and fit people on the planet!

Does God literally destroy us? No. However, He will not violate the laws He has laid out plainly for us to follow and obey...not for me...not for you...not for anyone. He does not violate our will, no matter how painful it is for Him to watch our life unfold, knowing the future that awaits us because of our wrong choices. We must take seriously what He takes seriously.

At the time, I couldn't see that sleeplessness was a serious omen of declining health. It never even crossed my mind that taking sleep aids for an extended period of time was in reality, defiling my body. Sadly, I was clueless and wound up on a long, winding slide to destruction that totally compromised my health. Little did I know that the warning signs were flashing all around, screaming desperately for my attention. Had I realized what I was doing to myself, I certainly would have thought more in terms of addressing the root issues instead of masking the symptoms.

The root problem was my obstinate refusal to ever completely unplug from my work. Even if your work is as important as ministry, if you ignore the basic laws of maintaining your health, you will cheat yourself, your family and the Kingdom of God of your greatest, most productive years. We live in a stressful world. Many people work heroically for what they consider to be important. I have the greatest respect and compassion for the thousands of achievers who are headed for that washed out bridge. For those who are either ignoring the signs, disregarding the warning signs all around or don't know what the signs are, this book is for you.

Some of you may have already passed the point of real danger making you and your family vulnerable, just as I did. I am hopeful that as you read on, you will begin to recognize where you are and will begin making the necessary adjustments. The message contained within these pages is a lifeline to pull you back to safety. As you continue reading, get ready to take hold of the lifesaver— simple principles that I pray will affect you enough to make you take immediate action to do whatever is necessary to preserve your life, health and emotional well-being.

No matter how hopeless the situation seems, I am proof you can make it through the valley of the shadow of death. Through making needed adjustments, you can live a long life. You can live and not die. You *can* experience joy and fulfillment again! You don't have to repeat the mistakes I made.

I have always had an aversion to being average. In the name of "working for God," I broke every speed limit and ignored every flashing warning sign, speeding swiftly ahead, straight into a dark, dangerous void. Once it became apparent to me that I was in real trouble, I seemed powerless against the force of the current. I could not rescue myself without outside intervention.

Chapter Three

Just Suck It Up

I had a three-week mission trip planned that was very important to me and long in the making. Years ago, Donna and I determined that each of our four sons, Jeff, Josh, Gabe, and Garrett, would go with me on a major mission trip when they turned thirteen. As parents, we felt this was a good way to help our sons take the focus off of the "all about me" attitude that's so common in those early teen years and imprint a vision of God's love for a lost and dying world on their hearts.

My first three sons had already taken their trips, and now it was my fourth son's turn. For several months, Garrett had been looking forward to this trip that spanned different continents. I had also been looking forward to it, yet at this time I was really dreading it. But I felt I absolutely had to go because I was honoring a family tradition that Donna and I had begun with our first son. I couldn't bring myself to back out.

My schedule had already been beyond my crazy "norm" in the preceding weeks. When Joyce Meyer asked me to accompany her to Dallas and Atlanta to appear on TBN with her, I didn't feel I should refuse. At that time, I was her pastor and wanted to help her in any way I could. It was a good trip, but I was exhausted the entire time. I did not sleep well, but unwisely attributed this to just getting over a bad case of the flu.

I was not looking at the big picture of my overall health. In fact, I saw each physical ailment as an inconvenient little speed bump. If you are like me, you hate to slow down for speed bumps, especially when you are in a hurry. *The only problem was, I was always in a hurry!*

Speed bumps are there for a reason—to purposefully make us slow down. Although commitment to the cause and heartfelt dedication are key elements of success, my unconscious motto to "just suck it up and keep going" could have easily been my demise. It never occurred to me that these speed bumps were indicators of an impending storm. In my weakened condition, after teaching in two services on Sunday, we went home to prepare to leave for our three-week mission trip. While Donna was packing our bags, I said to her, "I am in trouble, Donna. I feel like I do when I arrive home from a trip, and I haven't even left yet."

Donna knew how the flu had affected me and how tired I was and questioned whether or not I should go. Of course, I felt I had no option because of all the well-rehearsed reasons I had already run through in my mind. But I did have nagging doubts that were surfacing stronger now. In my reasoning process though, I rationalized the inner turmoil. On the one hand, I knew I was in no physical condition to go anywhere. On the other hand, I reasoned with myself and my wife that I had made this commitment several months prior, and many pastors and leaders were counting on me to be a part of this very important trip.

I chose to ignore the possibility that my gut feeling was God's attempt to warn me. Instead, I attributed the unrest to my concerns for Donna regarding the recent loss of her mother, along with my increasing concerns for my dad's failing health.

Donna's mother had lost the battle with cancer a couple of months before and Donna was still grieving the loss. My dad, who had been wonderfully healed of cancer during our church's revival period, had just found out that cancer had returned. He was not given a good prognosis. In addition to these things, the situation with our first son, Jeff, had gone from bad to worse. Then to top it off, one of my young staff pastors, a spiritual son who was converted and mentored under my ministry, had become offended and quit.

I felt an incredible amount of pressure from these situations, as well as many other things I had no control over. But as a man and a leader, I felt I must be strong and keep on going like I always did. Tragically, I was just not being honest with myself. After long conversations with hurting people, I realized that I was not the only one who had made these mistakes. When you are a very strong person, always able to deal with and handle anything and everything, it is really difficult to even consider being weak or not in control of your life.

Neither my wife, nor my dad, wanted me to stay home on their account because they were trying to do the same as me—"just suck it up." In other words, we were trying not to complain, but to be strong and just deal with it. The look of disappointment in Garrett's eyes at the mention of not going was enough to push me past all rational thought. So we loaded up and off we went.

Our first flight took us to Nairobi, Kenya for meetings with a dear friend in ministry. The meetings were wonderful and God graciously impacted the people there. I was treated to lots of local fish and game at a particular restaurant. (I only mention this because that fact came up a lot in future days when the infectious disease specialists were searching for a cause for my illness). We also spent some time visiting with a tribe of the famed Maasai Warriors of Kenya, often featured on the National Geographic Channel. This was a never-to-be-forgotten experience for both of us. Then Garrett and I boarded a plane and headed to India.

Ten thousand pastors came from all over India to be in this conference organized specifically for ministers. The conference was coordinated by Jack Harris of Global Messenger Service and sponsored by Joyce Meyer and her ministry. The three of us spoke to those wonderful pastors for five days and nights. It was amazing to see their hunger for God and their appreciation for the opportunity that brought so many of them together for the first time.

After that, we flew to Malaysia where Jack, my childhood friend and now a missionary based from our church had ministered and lived for several years with his wife and daughters. Then we made the long trip home—twenty-nine hours in the air, not counting layovers and plane changes. Once I stopped long enough to feel something, I realized that I was feeling really fragile.

When you are exhausted but insist on continuing at a non-stop pace, pushing through the tiredness, your body begins to run purely on adrenaline. Every hormone is regulated by adrenaline and every organ needs it to function properly. Simply put, the adrenal function is like a full glass of water. As you go through the day, experiencing challenges and stresses (whether good or bad), the glass is drained to the halfway mark.

When you get a good night's sleep, the glass is filled again, ready for the next day. But when stress is constant and sustained, sleeping becomes increasingly difficult because the sleep hormone is disturbed. Without the proper amount of restful sleep, the glass (your adrenal system) declines over time to a place where it stays around the half-full mark all the time. If the situation is not recognized and necessary adjustments made, any new stressors will be magnified, further depleting your energy level. Then sleep will become further disturbed and the adrenaline will fall below the half-full mark. At that point, your adrenaline level can deteriorate rapidly and exponentially until your glass is drained. Your body will then begin to extract adrenaline from organs in a desperate attempt to replenish what was withdrawn. Without extreme lifestyle changes, disaster is inevitable.

Taking Your Life Back

Chapter Four

The Dominos Begin to Fall

When Garrett and I returned home the day before Thanksgiving, I had a high fever and the skin over my entire body was alive with pain. Every touch felt like sandpaper on raw nerve endings. Thanksgiving dinner at my mother's house was cut short because I felt so weak. A couple days later, I broke out with an extremely painful rash. My wife pulled out all her medical reference books and decided the symptoms looked like shingles. All I knew was, it was bad and I was miserable!

Our trusted family doctor of many years retired during the time I was traveling internationally, so this added to the stress of the situation. It took great effort on my wife's part to get me worked into the replacement doctor's busy schedule. This new doctor took one quick, cursory look and said almost flippantly, "I have no idea what that rash is!" After glancing through my file he said, "I see you had a topical cream before, so I will write you another prescription. If this cream doesn't work, go see a dermatologist in a week or so. Nice to meet you…" and out the door he went.

The appointment that I was so desperate for lasted no more than five minutes. He didn't even ask any questions! I was bewildered and angry. My wife was furious. (I want to mention here that though I believe most physicians are devoted, caring professionals, there are a few who are not. The same could be said for ministers—or any profession for that matter.)

My pain increased daily. Donna didn't wait a week or so as the doctor had recommended, instead she called the very next day to schedule an appointment with a dermatologist. He was booked solid for weeks. We tried to get in on an emergency basis, but even those slots were filled. The receptionist said our only recourse was to wait for a cancellation or try to get an appointment with another doctor. The unrelenting pain and uncertainty of the situation only added to our stress and frustration.

In the meantime, I had Sunday services to prepare for. After returning from my overseas trip, I was already a few days behind in getting to the office to meet with my pastoral team and staff. I wanted to be brought up to date on any issues that had come up while I was away. There is usually something that needs urgent attention after a long trip like that.

My dad's declining health weighed heavily on my mind. My mom, Esther, has always been the most upbeat and cheerful person I know. It is a rare day indeed, when anyone she comes in contact with doesn't get a good dose of "happy" deposited in them by the encounter. When my mom gets even a little less outgoing, it is really noticeable. Even though she kept smiling, I could see what she was *not* saying in her eyes. I wanted so much to be able to do something to fix this situation so she wouldn't have to go through this.

During this time, I began to notice numbness in my hands and feet along with the pain I was experiencing. Just before Christmas, I was relieved to be notified that there was an opening with the dermatologist due to a cancellation. I had been waiting for five weeks for this appointment, and my condition had worsened considerably.

The breakout of shingles was at the base of my spine, causing the pain to travel through all the nerve endings in my body. I had a tremor in my hand and my balance was becoming unstable. It had become impossible to continue my schedule at work. I thought that maybe the dermatologist could give me some answers and do something to stop this agonizing pain.

When the doctor examined the rash, he said, "Oh! This is shingles." He ran out of the room and came back with a hypodermic needle in hand and promptly gave me a full injection. He said, "I hope this is not too late! It is supposed to be given at the onset of shingles to be effective against the virus. Without it, recovery is longer and more painful. The nerve damage can be long lasting or permanent."

Great! I thought sarcastically, remembering the nonchalant attitude of the first doctor. I had been suffering unnecessary agony for over five weeks! I could have had this medication the first week, if that doctor had cared even a fraction as much as this one! I was in so much pain; I couldn't tell what part of my body hurt the most.

I had a rush of intense anger toward the first doctor, but I didn't want to add this emotion into the mix with everything else so I forced myself to acknowledge the injustice, consciously forgive him and let it go. It was done and couldn't be undone. I needed to concentrate all my strength and energy on the present—doing whatever was necessary to recover.

The dermatologist asked me a lot of questions, shaking his head in disapproval as I told him what happened with the first doctor. He was concerned because the shingles had gone undiagnosed and untreated for so long. He prescribed a different cream to apply to the rash and told me to take life very easy. The doctor further explained that we would simply have to wait and see if there would be more physical ramifications for not getting prompt and proper treatment. He told me to schedule a follow up appointment with my primary care physician so he could keep a close eye out for any complications. With Christmas just days away, this meant searching for a doctor since I was unwilling to place my well-being into the hands of someone who was obviously not concerned about me.

Christmas has always been my favorite season. All year I look forward to the Christmas Eve Service, which has become such a wonderful tradition for the families of our church...including mine. My dad's condition being what it was, I wanted to make sure that *this* Christmas and *this* service was especially wonderful for him. The combined pressure of my own physical condition and that of my dad's, intensified the stress I was feeling as I strove to make the service perfect. It was a beautiful night, yet bittersweet because I knew that without a miracle, it would be my dad's last Christmas with us.

As the New Year began, I realized I was beginning to have balance problems. It seemed like my equilibrium was off; I would become dizzy and very weak at the slightest movement. When I sat for a while and stood, or when I stood for a while and tried to sit down or walk, my legs buckled. I was used to sitting down and getting up without conscious thought, but now that simple effort completely drained all the strength from my body.

I had never been weak like this a day in my life. I kept thinking to myself, *This is just a fluke—a passing after-effect of the shingles.* I began to get concerned, though, when the weakness didn't go away with the passage of time. Instead, it was progressively getting worse. I did everything I could to not let those around me see what was happening. As much as possible, I would simply wait until everyone was out of the room before I attempted to move or get up, and then I would take it very slowly.

My physical problems began to migrate into my spiritual life. After enjoying a beautiful relationship with God in prayer and His Word for many years, I could hardly pray now. I could barely get words out of my mouth. I found it difficult to read the Bible and I no longer seemed to be able to comprehend it. With my struggle for focus to pray and read, it became increasingly difficult to fight in faith for my healing. I was in a mess—*a real mess!*

I came to a place where I wasn't hearing from God. I began to pray, "God help me. God help me," because that was all I could pray. After two weeks, the Lord spoke to me and said, "I've heard your prayer. Now, change your praying. Ask Me instead to open your eyes." It was good to hear the voice of the Lord after such a long time. I began to pray, "God, open my eyes." After several weeks of praying this, He began to speak to me. I was able to read and comprehend more. At times, my brain was so foggy that I had a hard time assimilating my thoughts enough to communicate. I couldn't think coherently.

My ability to study and prepare a sermon for Sunday services was affected, but

I was fortunate to have a pastor on staff who was excellent at taking my scattered thoughts and capturing the heart of what I wanted to convey to my congregation. He did the research and helped me put the sermons in order. By the grace of God, I was able to use those notes to communicate what He had put into my heart. It was as if when I stood to speak, God's strength and ability came and carried me until I was finished.

As I walked to the back of the platform to go down the stairs and through the door to the room behind the stage, many times my legs would buckle before I got to the bottom of the stairs. . I felt like my body was that of a decrepit old man, yet I was only in my mid-forties! My staff always made sure I had two strong men to help me get to the room Then from there, I would sit and gather enough strength to go out to the car. After service, I went to our favorite restaurant with my family in order to keep things as "normal" as possible. But the effort of going out to eat and being around a lot of people and noise, in addition to the energy required for preaching, left me with no reserves to share in our usual jovial conversation.

I could not do anything with my family or at the office for an eighteen-month period. It seemed like a lifetime! I sat at home in a chair and couldn't even handle the excitement of watching a baseball game on television. When there were two outs and bases loaded, as normal as that is, it caused me great anxiety. At night, I would lay in bed hoping to fall asleep to escape the constant stress I felt about what I was going through. I was spinning on a downward spiral. At times there seemed to be no hope.

While all this was happening to me personally, my dad was fighting for his life. There were many times that he had my mom bring him to our house and we would pray because he felt like he was dying. We would pray until the feeling passed.

Sometimes, however, we had to take him to the emergency room. Then the doctor would give him medicine and after a while, we would all be able to go home. It was only later, after he passed, that we realized what had been happening to him. His experience helped me understand a lot about what was going on with me.

I went on for months not knowing what was really wrong with my body. This added to the anxiety I was experiencing. There are no words to describe the fear of the unknown. I went to the top neurologist in St. Louis, as well as to an infectious disease specialist. They all endeavored to pinpoint the reason for the neuropathies (a degenerative state of the nerves and nervous system) which they felt was the cause of the equilibrium problems I was experiencing, as well as the numbness and sudden weakness in my limbs. During further testing, they found that the numbness in my hands and feet had increased and progressed further up my arms and legs.

After researching known diseases and pathogens from the countries I had been to, one doctor thought I had an amoeba or parasite from the fish and game I had eaten in Kenya. Another doctor thought I was experiencing the side effects of shingles. In every diagnosis proposed, there were other physical issues that didn't fit in the description. As a result, none of the doctors could agree on a diagnosis.

One thing the doctors did agree on was the standard procedure of at least trying to control the symptoms with prescription medication until a solid diagnosis could be determined. I was first given Neurontin for the numbness and other nerve symptoms. The first dose knocked me out for a whole day. But after a few months, I could take the maximum dosage and strength without effect. I was frustrated, so I weaned myself off of this medication. (I do NOT suggest that you endeavor to wean yourself off of medicine without your doctor's knowledge.)

I was tired of experiencing all the side effects without making any real progress. I wasn't sleeping more than thirty-minute segments at a time throughout the night. Most nights were filled with long periods of sleeplessness in between sleeping. Many times in those dark night hours, I felt like I couldn't stand the situation anymore. That was when the strongest sleeping medications were prescribed for me. I just wanted to sleep.

I kept praying and speaking God's Word over my situation as much as I could with the fogginess in my thoughts. I was adamant about one thing—I was not going to become negative or speak negatively because I knew that life and death are in the power of the tongue (Proverbs 18:21). My trust was in God and His faithfulness to bring me through. Little did I know, all of my trust was about to be tested severely.

Chapter Five

Coming Unraveled

When the year 2000 rolled in, I entered one of the two darkest periods of my life. The world as I knew it, was crumbling all around me. The cancer had spread throughout my dad's body and reached his brain. He could no longer make decisions. On one of his better days, he told us he was at peace and ready to go. We had a family meeting and called hospice. It was incredibly difficult to do this, because we had really taken our stand against this disease in faith. Prior to my dad's healing of the first episode of cancer, I cried out to God to extend his life. The Lord graciously answered my request. I now continued to pray and speak healing over him in spite of the symptoms, just as I was doing for myself.

During that summer, my oldest son, Jeff, went missing in Nashville for several days. We were all frantic until he was found. He was safe, but not in good shape physically or spiritually and directed a lot of anger at us. It seemed like Donna and I kept having the breath knocked out of us by one terrible blow after another. Each blow hit us deeply and emotionally. Just as we gasped for a new breath of air, we were hit again repeatedly without a break from a completely different direction. There are many things that happened during these six years that I cannot, and will not, ever speak about. I will say, though, that there seemed to be a diabolical scheme of attacks designed to steal our hope and crush the very life and vision out of Donna and me.   But in these darkest of times, from deep within, we held onto the faithfulness of God and His love for us by a conscious decision of our wills. In times like these, God can seem far away and almost detached from our plight. These are the moments that put to the test all we say we believe about God and later, after coming through the difficulties, it makes our faith in Him even more unshakeable. Many times, though, this line is never drawn in the sand at the beginning of difficulties. This is what causes questions (Why? Why me?) to be directed at God out of unrelenting emotional and physical pain.

In the fall, Donna was desperate for a break and asked if we could go to a prophetic conference in Maui. So for her benefit, I reluctantly agreed. I had found out that simply sitting in meetings would weaken my system further so we compromised on the number of services I thought I could attend.

While attending the conference, we met and struck up an instant friendship with three of the speakers at the conference and spent time with them outside of the meetings. During a conversation with one of the speakers, we were asked us to tell about ourselves. In response to hearing what I was going through, Jim began to relate to me how he had faced a similar physical crisis. As he thoroughly described what he had experienced, I identified with everything and wanted to know what he had done to overcome it. *I was desperate to get well.* Jim told me the only thing that worked in the end was going away and taking a period of time off from any kind of ministry. That didn't seem to be an option for me, but I was very grateful for all he shared.

Just before we left to go home, two of the speakers, a husband and wife team, asked us to come to their room because they felt they had an encouraging word from the Lord for us. They shared many helpful things with us that day, but one thing they said caused Donna and I both to begin sobbing. This couple did not have any knowledge about our concerns for our son, Jeff. In fact, we had just met at this conference. Inspired by the Lord the wife said, "Your son, *your lost son*, will come to himself before the end of this calendar year. His eyes will be opened and he will come back and say to you, 'Mom, Dad, I am sorry for the hell I have put you through.'"

Upon hearing these words, our pain poured out through wailing and tears. The situation seemed impossible, but encouraged by this word, we were reassured that with God, nothing is impossible. When you reach the point where you think you can't go on, God will often bring a word of encouragement from another person that infuses you with strength. Hope for our son was renewed.

Our second son, Joshua, was getting married on October 24, 2000, to Tori, his childhood friend. We were so happy for him and tried not to let my health concerns put a damper on his coming celebration. At this time, another symptom surfaced that unbeknownst to me, was a precursor of terrible things to come. I found that I couldn't tolerate the emotions I felt in different circumstances, whether good or bad, happy or sad. It became a constant struggle to control my feelings in order to remain calm.

When we went out to lunch with Josh and Tori, naturally they would talk animatedly with enthusiasm about the upcoming wedding, Strangely, I found myself withdrawing. As thrilled and overjoyed as I was about their happiness, I couldn't handle expressions of emotion without feeling weak and drained. I found no answers in the constant search to understand why the expression of emotion would leave me feeling this way.

I absolutely could not tolerate noise *or* complete silence. I couldn't handle being in a room with a lot of people, but neither could I be alone. Donna had to always be within sight or calling distance. At that time and for years to come, what sent me to the brink was being told negative things—especially more than one bad thing in a given conversation. The words would slice right through me and I felt as if I were falling into a black pit. Looking back, I realize that this stemmed from feeling completely helpless to control anything concerning my own physical situation. Anything more was just too much to handle or deal with.

As a pastor, there is always something happening that can be taken negatively if you don't stay on top of it. People get offended or decide to leave the church without telling you—even when they have been there for years. Since you love them and are like a spiritual parent, it is like having a child walk away. There is a sense of loss and it causes pain every time. I am not one of those pastors who can have an "I don't care, let them go, good riddance" attitude. I take my calling and responsibility for the people God has blessed us with personally and very seriously.

One day, a long-time church member called to inform me that because I was sick, she was going to, in her own words, "jump ship." Instead of staying to be a help and strength through the crisis as a person of much prayer, she decided to leave because she felt our church would likely sink because of my illness and weakness. She didn't want to be there to watch it happen. I can't even say what that did to me…another gut punch. I don't know why we kick people to the curb when they are down.

The week before my dad passed, someone from the church insisted that I leave my dad's bedside to come to the office for a meeting. I had no idea what could be so important. When I arrived, the purpose of the meeting was to express disappointment in my leadership, itemizing all the things he believed I was doing wrong. I was devastated by the insensitivity. At the time, I realized that I already had too much to handle, so I forced myself to temporarily dismiss the issue in order to survive the next few weeks. I reminded myself over and over again that this person really had no idea of the struggle I was experiencing. I had no way of adequately explaining it either.

Remember this principle when you interact with others—there <u>are some things in life that you must experience for yourself in</u> <u>order to truly understand and have compassion.</u> Knowing this, and knowing he had never experienced any of what I was now going through, I chose to forgive and let it go. I knew my life depended on me keeping a constant vigil on the words that came out of my mouth, so in many situations where I normally would have spoken, I simply remained silent.

It's worth mentioning at this point, faith grows from the soil of love. Bitterness, unforgiveness, strife and self-pity are contaminants you cannot afford. People will disappoint you, but you must keep a positive outlook. Keep believing in people, but keep your faith rooted in God alone. Renew your commitment daily to forgive and love others as Jesus loves you. This is a vital key to good mental health, physical health, and spiritual health.

I spent as much time as I could physically handle with my mom and dad. For days we had kept a constant vigil by his bedside, but at the end of a very long evening, I felt I had to go home for a couple of hours to try to get some sleep. I had just gotten to bed when the call came to come back immediately, but I didn't make it in time.

Our son Jeff and his two cousins were sitting at the foot of my dad's bed when he suddenly opened his eyes and looked straight at each one of them before turning his face to the window. There were no curtains or blinds on it and he had often spoken staring out of that window and feeling the moon shining on his face while he prayed in the sleepless hours of the night. As the Lord shined on his frail body that night, He welcomed Dad home.

The experience profoundly impacted Jeff and his cousins because "Pawpaw" hadn't been conscious for days. That last look held all of the prayers they knew he had prayed for them and their walk with the Lord for as long as he was able to pray. His prayers were not in vain.

I felt the loss of my dad…too deeply for words. Just knowing that he wouldn't be there on the front row, always leaning forward, cheering me on with his "amen's" and encouragement was too much to process. I also knew that I couldn't just be his son at his funeral because I was also his pastor. I kept telling my wife, "Honey, if we can just make it through Sunday, I promise, on Monday we will take the week and rest."

The funeral was a fitting tribute to my dad. William E. Shelton, lovingly known as "Woody" by his friends, was a true servant of the Lord. Though facing his death was incredibly tough, our whole family was blessed by the overflowing support and love shown to us through that most difficult time.

We stayed with Mom until late Sunday night and went home in a drizzling rain. We were all exhausted. When Monday morning finally dawned, my wife got up to take the boys to school. She came in abruptly and asked, "Did you leave your car at your mom's?" I replied, "No, of course I didn't." I reminded her that we had all ridden back home in my car the previous evening. She then informed me that my car wasn't in the driveway. I wrongly assumed that she was just exhausted and confused.

She left again to take the boys to school in her car. Once again she rushed back in to tell me there were parts of my car at the entrance of our driveway. Someone had stolen the car and ran into the gate, leaving the side mirror and other small pieces scattered in the road. When the police officers arrived and were taking the report, a call came in that a car fitting the description of mine had been found in a ravine miles away. It seemed someone had followed us home and took my car for a joyride after we went to bed.

It was at this point that my wife lost it. Our home had been our only sanctuary and now, even that too had been violated. Later she was told by a friend that it was like the enemy marched right up to our door and mockingly said, "There is nothing you have that I can't get anytime...anywhere."

My sweet wife has the strength of steel in a crisis. I was leaning heavily on her throughout this time, so it was very hard for me to watch her strength crumbling before my eyes. I felt largely responsible. She cried for days. The car was not quite totaled, which meant a long, costly repair, and one more very hard circumstance with which to cope.

Chapter Six

Panic

In prayer one morning after the car incident, I was inspired to call Pastor Joel Osteen's brother, Paul, a friend and noted surgeon, to ask for help to find the best neurologist in the country. I cannot adequately convey with words my profound gratitude to Dodie, Joel and Paul Osteen for their graciousness to me at that critical time in my life. They were so encouraging to me over lunch, and Joel invited me to speak at the mid-week service of Lakewood Church. It was such an honor and was somewhat therapeutic for me, even though I felt I was fighting for my life at the time.

They took care of the arrangements so I could be examined by one of the top neurologists in the country at Baylor Neurological Hospital in Houston. For the first time in a very long time, I had a glimmer of hope. The neurologist Paul recommended was truly the best in his field. He was followed everywhere by a bevy of doctors and interns who hung on his every word, writing them down on their clipboards.

He took my medical history and then ordered a battery of rigorous tests and examinations that lasted five days. The last and most difficult test was the brain wave test, which was designed to bring out within the confines of this one test every bad neurological symptom I had ever experienced . Through it, he could measure the damage to my nerves and make a proper diagnosis. The good and bad part is that it worked…*all too well.* My nervous system couldn't handle the overload, and I began to feel as if I were going to die right then and there. This is when I experienced my first full-blown panic attack.

For years to come, I never went more than a day without experiencing at least one panic attack. Within a couple of weeks of the brain wave test, a situation I had to confront caused me to have an anxiety attack that lasted pretty much non-stop for two full weeks. Every waking moment, I struggled to control the waves of anxiety and fear and whatever sleep I was getting at that point vanished.

Sometimes people tell me that they think they may have experienced a panic attack. I always tell them, "If you *think* you've had a panic attack–you haven't." There is no way to explain the terror and feeling of utter helplessness during a panic attack. Everything in you, physically and mentally, is gripped by it.

When I met the doctor for the final analysis, he ruled out diseases like muscular dystrophy and a host of other major neurological diseases and disorders. Not satisfied, he asked if I would answer some personal questions. After I answered all of his questions, he put down his clipboard and just looked at me. He said he couldn't pinpoint the cause of my difficulties because there were so many.

Various factors and crises had all converged over the prior few years to bring me to this physical condition. It was also very possible that during the overseas trip I had been exposed to a pathogen, now untraceable, that still affected me. The emotional distress of my family situations only compounded all the other probabilities of what caused my sad condition. The doctor further explained that I had extensive nerve damage from shingles that would necessitate a period of years to repair and regenerate due to the extent of the damage…if ever it could be repaired. The only good news was that I was not terminal. The not-so-good-news was that he didn't have a concrete solution to my problem.

Though the doctor was very kind, his recommendation, based on his findings, was that I leave the ministry immediately for no less than two years and severely restrict all activity. I was to do nothing stressful during that time if I was to have any hope of progress. At that moment, my first glimmer of hope was completely snuffed out. I had never felt such despair. I felt like I was thrown into the ocean with my hands and feet tied…. Oh, God…

Everything he suggested, I informed him, was simply not possible for me to do. I realize now that taking this position was a huge mistake. When your body talks to you, *listen*! When someone who knows what they are talking about tells you what you must do to get well, *do it*! At that time, though, I was not prepared to leave my church, even in the hands of those I trusted. It wasn't that I thought I was so important; it was just that I couldn't conceive that this was what I was supposed to do. At that time, I didn't understand a principle that I now live by—*no one can afford to be too busy to do whatever is required to ensure they maintain or regain their health.*

After detecting my resistant attitude, the doctor suggested I take off at least one year. He then tried to convince me to consider a short sabbatical of at least three to six months, but my look told him that wouldn't work for me either. I could not wrap my brain around the details and ramifications of taking that much time off. A black pit of despair was clawing at my mind. It was hard for me to even think, much less process the scope of what he was telling me.

Finally, understanding that I was not going to be compliant, the good doctor gave his final advice. "Go home, find a doctor who will give you adequate medication to control your symptoms and pray for a miracle. You will need one." With that, I returned home. I had to perform my son's wedding that week in a way that would, under no circumstances, dampen the joy of the occasion. I felt responsible to be there for my mom, who had brought her own mother home to care for almost immediately after Dad's passing. Life had become an unforgiving and constant obstacle without reprieve. Perhaps that's the way life had always been, but I had finally arrived at a place physically and mentally in which I simply couldn't handle it.

I began to walk through each day, moment by moment, trying to not lose the tenuous grip I had on life. I felt I had been mowed down and buried under an avalanche of circumstances I could do nothing about. I was suffocating under the pressure, unable to face life, much less handle stress of any type.

At times I would improve slightly, but not much. As a result, not only was I suffering greatly, but my wife was suffering also. She became my caregiver. She was making up the difference in our family and ministry for what I could no longer do. Caregivers take on the extra burden of trying to cover for the afflicted in many different areas. This can become tedious, like walking on eggshells.

My children suffered too. They would tell you that for a number of years, I was not myself. It was very hard for them to see their dad, who had always been strong and fun-loving, reduced to a mere shadow of the man he had once been.

I now know personally the range of emotions that people experience when they suffer prolonged illnesses. I now know what it is like to feel separated and detached... knowing that most people cannot understand what you are going through.

For six years I felt like I was standing aloof, looking from a distance at everything that was going on. I would become quiet in situations where I previously would have been talking animatedly, dreaming and planning for the future. I didn't talk much because I was desperately trying to control the rising panic and anxiety that contemplating the unknown future brought. I would have to leave almost every social setting because stimulation of any kind was completely unbearable.

All of the stressful things happening in my life were actually adding to the decline of my health. I had begun to realize that mental stress and pressure can rob a person of their very life. At times, I felt like I could not go on. But, because of my knowledge of God's Word and because I am such a positive person by nature, I hardly ever allowed myself to speak negatively. It was a discipline that I became very strict and rigid about. I knew how very important the words were that I spoke, so I endeavored to be positive in my thoughts and words. However, during this very difficult time of my life, I began to get worn down. As a result, I came to my wife on two occasions and said, "I just don't know if I'm going to make it." Within moments after I spoke those words, I said, "Please God, forgive me, I'm sorry. I can't believe I just said that. Of course, I'm going to make it. You've told me that I will never experience anything that's beyond my ability to overcome with Your help.

As an exercise of controlling what I could control, I began a conscious habit of telling myself constantly, "If you can hold on and make it through the rest of this day, you will be all right. If you can make it through this service and deliver your heart to your congregation, you will be all right. If you can make it through the next hour to bedtime, maybe you will sleep and then you will be all right." This went on and on for six years.

Chapter Seven

The Lost Years

Over the course of time, I was given diagnoses of, but not limited to, adrenal exhaustion, nerve damage, measles, insomnia, panic/anxiety disorder, and various other active viruses in my nervous system. I had already been taking the strongest sleep medicine that could be prescribed. Added to that were anti-anxiety medicines that were regularly increased in dosage until I was maxed out on them as well. I entered a time that I refer to as "the lost years." There is a lot about those years that I simply don't remember.

Every day was a fight to survive. I grasped for every offer of help like a drowning man. During this season, I was offered help from an organization that said they wanted to come alongside to strengthen and help me, promising they would never attempt to take over my church.

At this point, I feel I must share some of our history to help you understand why this whole situation nearly sent me over the edge. Life Christian Church was not birthed just because I wanted to start my own church. If that were the case, then joining this organization wouldn't have been such an issue. It may have even seemed the smart thing to do, given the seriousness of my physical situation. As it was, we wanted the help and fellowship they offered, but we didn't want to give up control over our destiny as a church.

I had been called to preach and pastor in a supernatural way and the church was begun in the same manner. I was given a supernatural vision from the Lord in March of 1979, as a young twenty-five year old man. I was at a conference and after one of the evening services I lay in bed praying. All of a sudden, I opened my eyes and began to see the first vision I had ever experienced.

The vision began with me looking at a sea of humanity. There were people as far as the eye could see. They were all sitting in chairs with Bibles, listening as I taught the Word of God. They had notebooks on their laps and were taking notes as I spoke. Down one aisle there were stretchers with sick people on them. Down the other aisle there were people in wheelchairs. In one moment, the people in the congregation spontaneously got up out of their chairs and began ministering to the sick all around them. Across that vast sea of humanity, the hurting people began to get up and rejoice because they were now healed.

In awe, I asked the Lord what this vision meant. He replied, "This is a church, *My church*, and I want you to pioneer and pastor it. If you will be faithful and obedient, all that you see will come to pass."

"Where?" I asked.

"St. Louis," He replied.

I was just a young man, not very experienced in ministry, yet I knew this was a most holy thing and must be treated with utmost reverence. That is why and how Life Christian Church began and why it is still a vital presence in our city today. So, during those "lost years" of my illness, I struggled to make the best decisions possible, always keeping in mind the most holy charge the Lord gave me after the vision. My heart has remained constant in its commitment to be obedient to God, regardless of personal cost.

Regrettably, some decisions proposed by the organization would never have been approved if I had been well and thinking properly. Undoubtedly, I hurt people I loved in the process and for that, I am truly sorry. Even with all that, there were times when I felt I was making real progress. There were even seasons when it seemed all was on the mend, even though I still had anxiety attacks and was unable to sleep through the entire night. Those brief seasons of improvement gave me great hope that the end was in sight and that this terrible ordeal might soon be over.

Any progress achieved was short-lived, a week or two at most. Every time I felt I was 75, 80, or even 90% better, any crisis or problem in my church or family would wipe it all away. Consequently, the cycle of increased anxiety and sleeplessness would worsen, usually with another physical ailment arising. Each time this cycle repeated, the fight to keep hope that I would become well again became a greater struggle.

Looking back, I realize that it had been so long since I felt normal that I forgot what normal was. It is amazing how a person subconsciously adapts in order to cope with what they are going through. This is how they survive. I had learned how to adapt but didn't realize that this adaptation was a crucial factor hindering my ability to recover. Adapting to that kind of situation is dangerous because a person begins to change the ideal of what they expect out of life. When one settles for so much less than God's best because they are so beaten down by their circumstances, they begin to lose the strength of one of God's greatest gifts to humanity...*the will.*

With each setback came a gnawing fear that my life would never improve, that the suffering would never end, that this was just the way my life would be from here on. At first, I stood strong against this fear, but time after time I would wind up back at the brink of that black pit of hopelessness and despair. I resisted the fear, but with decreasing boldness. I couldn't even convince myself that this weakness could be conquered.

How does one cope? Some patients are given a terminal prognosis and promptly begin to fight it with all their might, not allowing for the possibility of death. It has been noted that in some of those cases, the person recovers and goes on to live a long and fruitful life. In other cases, patients are not given a terminal prognosis, yet their health begins to decline until they eventually die. Both scenarios are most puzzling to doctors.

God has blessed us with incredible instincts and the will to survive the toughest, most hopeless situations. Jesus paid the price for our healing, but ultimate victory lies with us. I had determined early on that I would not give up. I had seen too many instances of

God's power to heal.

Once I prayed for a dead baby that was brought to a crusade in Africa, and witnessed God restore her to life. Another time, a man came for healing and while waiting for prayer, he had a heart attack and died while in the prayer line! After prayer, he too was restored to life. I have seen blind eyes opened, deaf ears unstopped, tumors fall off and more diseases cured than I can count. *So...what about me?*

God is faithful to His Word and His promises regardless of our circumstances, whether good or bad. During the most difficult years of illness, even the lost ones that I cannot remember much about, with all the ups and downs, progression and setbacks, I wish I could say that I was a tower of strength and determination. Some days were filled with vision and purpose, while others I just struggled to make it through the day. God is not intimidated by our humanity or our weakness; He remembers that our physical frame is dust (see Psalm 103:14).

Taking Your Life Back

Chapter Eight

Desperation

In the two years before I experienced healing, it became evident that I would not get well without taking extended time off. I had to come to the place where I acknowledged that fact. Out of sheer desperation, I knew I was going to have to take a sabbatical. There was no other choice. I could no longer pastor the church. This was the second of my two lowest points in this whole scenario.

My team and the organization I was affiliated with came up with a solution I felt I could be comfortable with. The year 2005 would mark the 25th anniversary of Life Christian Church. We were going to make this anniversary a major event to celebrate the occasion. After much discussion, we came up with a plan to take a one-year sabbatical immediately following the 25th anniversary celebration. Donna and I would take a sabbatical for the sole purpose of healing my body by restoring my nervous system. I was adamant that I would only take this time off with the blessing of my congregation.

We had navigated several transitions to try to help me get well. Some of them were successful and several were not. At this point, I have to say how incredibly blessed I am with the quality of people who stuck with me through the good times and bad, who held to the vision of Life Christian Church as their own. They deserve a reward greater than I will ever be able to repay.

At one particular Sunday service in the early summer of 2005, Donna and I stood before our congregation and asked them for their blessing to take this sabbatical. We told them it would begin the day after the 25th Anniversary Celebration that was scheduled to happen on August 14th. We informed them that their blessing meant we would be gone for a year in order to do as the doctor had advised us to do several years ago.

My physical situation had turned for the worse and I saw no other option. However, without my congregation's blessing, I wouldn't go regardless of what that might mean to me physically. Most of the congregation rose to their feet in support. Some told me later, they were afraid of what a whole year would look like without me there. I felt we had only been limping along with me in this condition and wanted desperately to be able to move us forward with restored strength, vitality and vision.

The one thing Donna and I promised our congregation as we stood before them was that we would absolutely come back. We assured them that this was not a way of transitioning us out as many of them might fear.

During that time, along with everything else I was dealing with, I began to lose weight. I wasn't able to eat without discomfort, so I just quit eating except when I absolutely had to. When Donna began noticing the weight loss, she insisted I find out what was going on so we would know what to apply our prayers and faith to. The doctor wasn't happy with the rapid weight loss either, and told me I now had ulcers…another thing to deal with. I wondered at times if I would even live long enough to go on sabbatical to get well.

With the decision made that we would leave in August, Donna and I had to decide where to go and what to do to make the time conducive to recovery. A ministry friend of ours wanted me to go to a doctor who had treated him and his wife for exhaustion. I was open to any help from a friend, so I went for a consultation.

The doctor ran a lot of tests and was the one who discovered some of the active viruses working against my immune system. After finishing a lengthy medical questionnaire and answering many more questions about the previous years, he said he had a protocol that would help tremendously, but it wouldn't be easy or fun. He also said the sabbatical was good because the protocol would require constant attention, and that I would feel much worse before I felt better. Only the hope of getting "better" gave me the courage to face the "feeling worse" part. His prediction was an understatement. A few weeks after beginning the protocol, I felt like I was going to die. There are no words to describe the inner conflict occurring inside me leading up to the time we left for sabbatical.

As any true pastor knows, teaching becomes an integral part of your identity and purpose. I had never felt so vulnerable. The conversation in my head went something like this: "Am I making the right decision? Of course I am. I am physically unable to go on. But is there some other course of action I am not seeing besides going on sabbatical for a year? If there is, please let me know now!"

On and on this inner conflict continued, right up until the day we drove away. How does a pastor leave the church that he has poured his whole life into for twenty-five years? How does he respond to the tearful responses? "I don't know what I will do if you are gone for a whole year. You are my pastor! The only reason I am staying is because you promised you will come back!"

As a shepherd over my flock, although a very sick and weak one, my heart longed for my congregation. For months before I left , I went over scenario after scenario of what it would be like to be gone from them for that long. I had made many trips and had been gone for almost a month, but never, ever for a whole year. One year was unthinkable. I felt a tremendous weight of responsibility for my church's welfare.

Pastors know all too well that many people have difficulty adapting to good changes, much less something as radical as having their pastor be absent for an entire year. I spent a lot of time on my face in prayer over that. In whose care do I leave the church I was given by the Lord? Into whose care do I entrust the precious people who had been entrusted to me? I honestly felt that there was only one person with whom I could safely leave my congregation—my senior associate of many years. I felt he was the one person that our people would feel most secure with during our absence.

In addition, I had a good, strong leadership team of pastors that had been by my side for many years. In that, I found comfort in knowing that the people and the church would be cared for properly. There were endless details to be decided upon for the church, for my sabbatical, and for the upcoming 25th Year Anniversary Celebration that was fast approaching. I do not remember much about the time before I left because I was in such bad shape physically, mentally and emotionally.

When the big day finally arrived for us to begin our sabbatical, both Donna and I were nearly basket cases. Leaving was by far the hardest thing we had ever done. Only the knowledge that my body was shutting down kept us from backing out altogether. Not one person, not even my mom or my kids, knew how badly I was doing physically. It was another, "If I can just make it through this day, I will be okay" days.

It turned out to be a wonderful celebration with many of our dearest friends present. We were so blessed that Dave and Joyce Meyer and their whole family took time out of their busy travel schedule to be with us, as well many others who had been launched into ministry from Life. We laughed and cried at the pictures from the past and rejoiced in all that God had done in bringing us this far.

On the other hand, it was all I could do to physically endure all the excitement of the event. It took all the strength I could possibly muster to get through the celebration. Then, it was time to say goodbye. There were many tears as we thanked our church for the privilege and honor of being their pastors and for the gift of this sabbatical that they had so graciously given us so I could get well. We were presented with gifts and a wooden chest filled with notes and letters to be read when we were on our way. *We felt so loved.*

Unbeknownst to me, I was entering into the second darkest period of my life. Were it not for the prayers of my faithful friends and family, there is no way that I would have made it through that dark valley. What stretched before us was vast, uncharted territory. Donna and I had no experience with what lay before us. Tomorrow we were leaving everything and everyone that was familiar to set out into this time for my body to be restored to health.

What would that look like? We had no idea! Truthfully, it was a scary venture. You can't prepare for something like that in any way—it was a whole year of the unknown. We had faith and hope for a good outcome…*but no guarantees.* This was the biggest step of faith we had ever had taken and everything, our whole life and ministry, was on the line. Leaving made us feel like our hearts were being ripped out.

It was like being on a narrow path, high on a cliff, with room enough to only put one foot in front of the other. One false move and certain death awaits below. The path bends ahead so you can't see if there is danger in front of you. The only thing you do know is that eventually the path may lead to a better place than where you now stand. Turning back is not an option. Desperation forced us to continue and we had no choice but to go forward.

Chapter Nine

When Healing Hurts

After hugging and kissing our family goodbye, on Monday morning we headed west. One thing Donna and I had prayed about and knew for sure was that we had to go far enough away that if something came up with the church, we couldn't just run right back to take care of it.

I knew it would take weeks, if not longer, to detach myself enough that every other thought wasn't for my church and for all that was happening there. As a pastor, this concern was as much an unconscious part of me as breathing. Not knowing what was going on at church felt like when you are under water too long and desperate for air. Come to think of it, that was partly why I was in this situation. No one's body or mind is made to handle continuous pressure with no let up.

When my parents had taken my grandmother into their home, becoming her primary caregivers, it nearly wrecked my dad's health. His doctor insisted that the stress of the continuous care required by his mother who suffered from Alzheimer's, caused Dad's health to fail. Often, people in vastly different situations wonder why they feel so bad all the time but they never stop long enough to take inventory to see what could be causing their malady. So many things became clear to me after the fact. My discoveries birthed a passion to help others avoid the dangerous paths that nearly destroyed my life.

It was no easy task to pull our thoughts away from our beloved family and church, even as the miles away from them grew. This was especially true on the second day when Donna felt we were far enough away to open the box and read all the notes and cards. We basked in the love and encouragement, our eyes wet with tears. Their encouraging words became something we clung to in the dark days that were ahead.

I immediately began the protocol that was given to me by the doctor. Just as he had said, it required constant attention to take the right things at the exact time and in the prescribed amounts six times daily; in addition to the medicine I was using to control the panic and anxiety. The protocol also included taking natural liquids designed to restore my failing immune system as well as kill the viruses and bacteria that were attacking my organs.

If I had not left the church when I did, I would have died. *My body was shutting down.* The doctor said that after two weeks, I would feel better than I had in years... for about five days. Then, he said, I would feel like I had the worst case of flu I had ever had in my life. He further explained that the weakened state would continue as the junk that was alive and operating in my body was destroyed and purged. I had no idea that the cleansing process would be so difficult and that my body would ache and hurt continually.

We finally arrived in South Dakota where our dear friends,

Jack and Sherry Harris were waiting to meet us. We spent a couple days with them visiting historic places such as Mt. Rushmore and the monument to Crazy Horse. While Sherry and Donna strolled around taking pictures, Jack graciously kept me company on the nearest benches that we could find. I was exhausted after walking from the parking lot through the entrances. It wasn't really warm in South Dakota, even in August, and I just couldn't take the cool temperatures. The chill went right through me.

We were supposed to go together to Yellowstone National Park, but I told Jack and Sherry that I just couldn't. I had to get warm. We said our goodbyes and parted ways. Jack and Sherry continued without us and Donna and I headed south to the sun and warmth I desperately hoped awaited us.

When we called home to talk to the kids, it was very difficult to not ask how everything was going at the church. Many times daily, Donna and I would have to stop each other from unconsciously beginning a conversation about church matters. This presented a real challenge that we weren't being too successful at mastering. But for my health's sake, we knew we had to do this.

We finally arrived at a place that was warm. When the temperature rose to over a hundred degrees and didn't come down, we had to move again. It became apparent that my body could not tolerate cool temperatures or extreme heat either. It was depressing not to be able to find a resting place. Finally, we packed up and drove over the mountain to a place that was ten degrees cooler into an environment that was just right.

I had taken my motorcycle with us so I wouldn't have to unhook the motor home every time we needed to get groceries or go somewhere locally. After a short trip into town, I was so weak that I couldn't hold the bike up when we stopped. The bike leaned and the hot pipe began to burn my leg. Donna jumped off to help hold the bike up until I could get off. I nearly passed out from the pain. Finally we were able to secure the bike and I limped to a chair. Donna rushed to the first aid kit and said that the burn might be third degree in the center. The burn hurt badly for hours and it took weeks to heal. We prayed over my leg and did all we could with the first aid supplies we had. I just couldn't believe that had happened! I didn't get on my motorcycle again for a long, long time.

We had been on the sabbatical for a month and I thought surely, after one month, I would see some noticeable progress in my health, but I didn't. As September turned into October, the enemy began to tell me, "Well, now you're *never* going to get well, because if you were going to get well, wouldn't it have happened after one year or two years or three? Especially since you've been off on sabbatical these months, you should be getting better. You're *never* going to get better. You're *never* going to be able to continue ministry. Your life is over! Your purpose is over! *Everything* is over now." The enemy's momentum grew while my condition continued to decline.

I was supposed to be on a sabbatical to get better, but like the woman with the issue of blood, instead of getting better, I grew worse (Mark 5:25-34). Can you imagine the hopelessness of my situation? I had been off for a handful of months, and yet I grew worse rather than better. My situation seemed hopeless. Many people back home thought I was having a great vacation, but I was battling for my very life.

How do you fight when you feel the fight going out of you? I knew I had to keep on doing what I was doing—spending the morning in prayer and study as I had done for years. I had to fight to keep a positive outlook when everything in my body seemed to be going further downhill. Even the promise from the doctor that feeling worse meant all the poisons in my body were being purged, did not help. I was becoming desperate for a change for the better.

I called home regularly to check on family and just to hear familiar voices. I was hungry to hear them tell me about normal everyday situations with the family and my grandson, Miles. When we asked my mom and our sons how everything else was going, their hesitancy to answer gave us cause for concern…especially mom's silence. Finally, after much prodding and explaining to them that their not saying anything left too much up to our imagination, they gave us the shortest and best version possible.

After hearing what they said, I felt like a knife was in my gut, but as always, I chose to believe the best. I tried to reassure my family as much as I could without being there. After all, I had left the acting pastoral team with clear instructions that they could do whatever necessary to move things forward, but could not make any major changes without notifying me first. I trusted them to do that. I was going on sabbatical to get healed, but didn't resign my authority under God as pastor. In the eyes of God, I was still ultimately responsible to Him for the church He had given me to pastor.

Donna and I had to really take charge of our thoughts and not let our imagination run away from us. We trusted our friends, and we trusted God. It was a severe test of our commitment to stay uninvolved so that I could get well.

In early October, Donna and I were both very restless and homesick and wanted to be with our family. I wanted to see familiar places and faces, at least for a week or two. We prayed and decided to go home for a couple of weeks, after which we would head east to Virginia so Donna could spend some time with her dad. She also wanted the opportunity to take pictures of the leaves turning colors, which Virginia is known for. We thought it would be a good, restful trip because it was familiar to us.

I had come to realize along the way that "new and different" came with its own amount of stress. At first the traveling was great. I have always loved seeing and discovering new things, but soon the traveling began to wear on me greatly. At any rate, I had become desperate to go home, sleep in my own bed, hug my mom, kids and grandson, and have someone encourage us.

Chapter Ten

Calm Before the Storm

We made it home from out West and as we anticipated, sleeping in our own bed and seeing our kids and grandbaby was just as wonderful as we had thought it would be. Even though everyone was happy to see us, we sensed an underlying tension and felt, there was something we were not being told. Because of my condition and wanting to protect Donna, I fought the urge to probe in order to find out what was really going on. Every day was still a fight to keep the darkness at bay and we maintained a strict vigilance on our words and thoughts.

As Donna and I practiced living every day with thankfulness, even in our darkest moments, we read, re-read and spoke out of our mouths this truth: God will never allow you to face any trial that is more powerful than the way of escape He has provided. He promised this in His Word (1 Corinthians 10:13). I clung to this truth many times when I thought I couldn't take any more. In those moments there would be a short break in the constant onslaught, as if angels had their arms and wings spread over us to hold back the hordes of relentless attackers. People from our past, as well as ministers we barely knew, would call or write to let us know that we had been heavy on their hearts and they had been covering us in prayer.

The greatest encouragement of all was when pastor friends let us know that they had led their church in prayer for us. It was comforting in those times when we felt so alone in our suffering to know that God in His mercy was calling on obedient people from many different places to be strong on our behalf and to hold us up in prayer. Jeff and Patsy Perry, fellow pastors in our city, are just one example of that kind of love. We are so thankful to God for them.

There were words from the Lord, given to us from ministers that were "just in time" words of encouragement. They gave us the boost we needed in times when we found ourselves with no more strength and at a loss for what to do next. While we were home, we avoided driving by the church lest we be tempted to go in. It was really difficult not to go to the church and certainly a test of our faith because of what we were sensing. We had to trust God completely with our church at this time.

Once again, we loaded up and drove to Virginia after kissing our loved ones goodbye. Our time in Virginia was very enjoyable, restful and peaceful. As we had anticipated, the colors of the leaves were especially beautiful that Fall. During that trip, Donna took some of her best pictures ever.

I still felt very ill every day, but while I was there in Virginia, the anxiety attacks lessened in severity and frequency. That was a great relief. I had some wonderful times in prayer and fellowship with God and He vividly brought back a scripture He had given me when I was out West. I spoke this scripture aloud and prayed it almost daily. "O God, You have taught me from my youth, and hitherto have I declared Your wondrous works. Yes, even when I am old and gray-headed, O God, forsake me not, [but keep me alive] until I have declared Your mighty strength to [this] generation, and Your might and power to all that are to come" *(*Psalm 71:17-18 Amplified Bible).

I held to the seventy-first Psalm to give me hope in my most hopeless, desperate moments. I clung to this scripture and declared that I would live and not die, as it seemed I was about to do. By the middle of November, Donna and I felt like it was time to go home. We had never been away from our family during Thanksgiving and Christmas holidays, and we especially didn't want to be away now. We made plans for the holiday season with our family and this gave us a lot of enjoyment during the long drive home.

It was good to enjoy creating some new memories on that Thanksgiving to ease the memory of the two previous, very difficult ones. And, even as weak as I felt, I became as excited as was physically possible about the quickly approaching Christmas season…something I always looked forward to. For me, the holiday season is all about giving and "good will to all men." I love all the celebration and decorations that go along with the holiday. I am so glad for the time of calm I had before the storm that nearly killed me.

Taking Your Life Back

Chapter Eleven

Rescued

I didn't foresee what happened next. I was completely unprepared and unable to sort it out. I may never be able to understand. It is a blur in my memory of pain and grief. In December 2005 and January of 2006, I took a turn for the worse. Mounting circumstances coming from all sides at once hit me hard. The slow progress from the medical protocol I had worked so diligently on for my body's healing was wiped out by the storm in a single week.

Panic and anxiety returned with a vengeance, stronger than ever before. Sleep completely escaped me. The ulcers that had been healing flared up with fury. It seemed a huge dark cloud of depression would swallow me. In all my years of life and ministry, I never imagined that I would experience anything of this magnitude. I felt like David facing Goliath, but without a slingshot.

I stopped the protocol. I knew that I was now fighting for my very life. The protocol wouldn't rescue me now. I prayed and prayed for God to show me His will and what to do. I was putting one foot in front of the other and trusting that God would get me through each day. Our family went to the Christmas Eve Service at our church without us. This is my favorite service of the year and of all the messages I preach, telling the story of our Savior's birth in a fresh way is the moment I enjoy most.

That night, Donna and I sat at home and tried to sing the carols they were singing at the church. We burst into tears and just held each other and wept as we sat on the piano bench together. This was the first Christmas Eve Service we had ever missed. The circumstances that led up to that night I will not speak of, but I felt like I had walked into an ambush of the enemy from which there was no escape. I had never felt so alone and abandoned in my life. I wasn't sure I had even a shred of hope left to hang onto...*I really felt at that moment I was dying.*

In January 2006, I was scheduled to go to a conference. I arrived a couple of days early to rest, pray and to be alone with God. Donna would join me in a few days, but I was so filled with anxiety, I didn't want to be alone for one moment. I forced myself to wait until later in the day to call her. Though at first I tried to sound nonchalant and casual, finally I told her I was counting the hours until she arrived. I knew she understood what that meant, but we both tried to keep it together until she could get to me.

I was so relieved when she finally arrived. It was a warm day, so I suggested that we take our books and go out by the pool for a while. After reading a book intently for some time, Donna handed it to me and said, "Rick. You *have* to read this chapter—*all the way through!*" Something in the way she said it made me know this was very important to her, and that I needed to give my full attention to what she wanted me to see.

We had owned this book that suddenly arrested her attention for many years. I was somewhat surprised that she was reading this particular book because it was not an easy or fast read, and certainly not something you would take to the pool to relax with. Yet, I was interested in what had so impacted her. The book had been written over one hundred years ago.

I took the book and read the chapter she had marked for me. The chapter was entitled "Passivity." The whole chapter described my experience perfectly. It seemed to be describing *me*—even to the fine details regarding my inability to make a decision. Decision making had become paralyzing to me. (I later learned this was another symptom of burnout.) I relied on others to make decisions. This was totally uncharacteristic of me prior to being ill.

Here I was, unable to make a decision for myself. I wouldn't take a risk. I was afraid of making a mistake. I had to have people help me think about everything. I didn't want to do anything independently. Everything seemed scary to me. Life had become a torment.

When I read this chapter, it described me to a tee. The truths in that one chapter seemed to unlock something within me. God gave me an understanding that suddenly caused me to see clearly what the real problem was. It opened the door for the breaking off of all the junk that had plagued me for over six years. Through that book, I suddenly understood what the root of my problem really was. *The spirit of fear had crept into my life.*

I would have never guessed the root issue was fear. Because I had never been a fearful person, I failed to recognize fear when it slowly and subtly crept into my life. It is possible for a person who is rarely afraid of things, to come under the influence of an invisible entity. Fear can affect you in ways you probably have never imagined. People often look for some complex answer to their seemingly complex problem. However, most of the time we miss the real issue, which is typically something simple and elementary. Later, we wonder how in the world we could have gone so long without seeing what should have been so obvious. "My people are destroyed for lack of knowledge" *(*Hosea 4:6*)*.

I am not recommending that you go on a witch hunt. You shouldn't. If you honestly enquire of your Heavenly Father, He will show you and make sure you understand the root of the problem. With the condition I was in, I could not see clearly.

God used a chapter in this out-of-print book to cause me to see principles that literally opened the door for me to receive my healing and the freedom I now enjoy. The main principle of the chapter on passivity that applied to me was that when the battle is long and intense; the ploy of the enemy is to convince us to change our stance. His aim is to stop us from believing and fighting fiercely with prayer and the confession of God's Word. His tactic is the subtle, ongoing bombardment of thoughts that we are not recovering or will never be the same again. In my case, this was the entrance of the spirit of fear.

Fear can affect you in ways you probably have never imagined. We are called to live by faith, not fear (Romans 1:17). Scripture tells us that the just shall live by faith." Second Timothy 1:7 says, "For God has not given us a spirit of fear, but of power and of love and of a sound mind." I want you to understand that anxiety is actually fear. Anxiety is another word for fear. The Lord spoke to me that day at the pool and said, "Rick, you have a spirit of fear. You have become lethargic and depressed in this whole battle. You must rise up and attack this spirit of fear."

On January 27, 2006, twelve days after reading the chapter on passivity, a ministry couple we trusted completely spent the day with us praying and speaking the Word of God over my situation. That evening, I asked the Lord to forgive me for allowing fear to rule me, even though I had not been aware of it until recently. Then, together with my wife, we rebuked the spirit of fear and commanded it to leave me in the Name of Jesus.

You may wonder, *Could my freedom come just that easily?* Yes. But you must understand and grasp something that is very important to your deliverance in whatever situation you are currently battling. Look at it this way, if the bull ever realized that the enemy was not the red cape being waved in front of his face but the matador waving it, he would never allow himself to be slaughtered. In the same way, when you see beyond the battle (red cape) you are facing and realize who the true enemy is who is trying to distract you from the real issue (your stance of faith), at that moment, the tide of the battle changes in your favor. You have just been awakened out of the lethargy that the ongoing circumstances and the intense physical battle have lulled you into, so that you can see the real truth of what is going on in your situation. It is such an "Ah-ha!" moment that all the previous self-doubt and questioning is replaced with confidence and faith.

The enemy functions in darkness, and when the true root of the problem is brought into the light and you see it for what it is, the enemy loses the advantage he has been holding over you. We rebuked that spirit of fear, and God delivered me. I am not saying that every symptom left on that day—that was not the case—but freedom was birthed within me. I knew I was free deep within my heart and that knowing caused me to have great confidence that my body would have to come in line.

For several days after that, periodically I continued to experience anxiety attacks. It's difficult to explain. Though this was occurring in my body, my spirit had become strengthened profoundly. I was aware of what was happening in a new way. I looked at my situation from a whole different perspective than I had just a few days prior. I was aware of the fact that fear had no more authority and power over me. The spirit of fear had moved out of my house. I was no longer afraid of the panic attacks. I was no longer afraid of being afraid. My confidence and excitement began to grow.

Five days later, on February the 1st, the Lord said, "Now, get rid of all the medication you've been taking for these six years." Let the record reflect, I'm not telling you to do this. Please understand this. It is very dangerous, even life-threatening to stop taking some prescription medications (especially strong, addictive medicines) suddenly. I would never have done so, except for a very definite instruction to do this from the Lord. Let me again repeat, stopping your medicine presumptuously could be disastrous for you. God rarely works the same way with everyone because of the uniqueness of each person's battle.

It's important to understand my track record with God. I've known the voice of God for many, many years and was confident He had spoken to me. On that day, I disposed of the pills—all of them. Amazingly, just before I did this, a spirit of fear tried to return. (You must realize that I could hardly sleep even three to four hours in a row *with* the sleeping pills, so disposing of them meant there would be nothing in the natural to help me sleep at all.) I almost started shaking with fear before I disposed of the medications, but I recognized what was happening. I said, "Devil, get out of here. I am already free. I do not have to worry about not sleeping, I can trust in the grace of God for that."

Afterward, it wasn't as if the symptoms suddenly changed, but the grace of the Lord came into my life like a warm blanket over my soul. There is a definition of grace I have compiled after much study. Grace is: God's empowering Presence to be all He has called me to be and to do all He has called me to do. This is the definition I use when I refer to grace in my messages.

That first night, I slept about forty-five minutes total. When I got up, I went all day dealing with many things at the church, yet feeling as if I had received adequate sleep the night before. The next night, I slept ninety minutes and had the same experience of being rested all that day also. The third night, I slept for four hours straight. On the fourth night, I slept seven hours and I've been sleeping all night ever since

It's not because I've had easy days since then; it's by the peace and grace of the Lord Jesus Christ. Even on the most challenging days, I go to bed and sleep seven to eight hours and it is because of God's healing grace.

I want you to know and understand that no matter how desperate things are in your life today-no matter how severe your situation becomes—you can turn it around. If you will ask the Lord to show you what the *real* source of your problem is, *believing He wants to reveal it to you.* He will show you and will set you free.

The enemy will lie to you incessantly. The enemy kept telling me during all the years of my illness, "It will never turn around. You'll die with this infirmity." Other times, he suggested something even worse. He suggested that I would grow old in this condition. There was a nagging insinuation deep within that my ministry was now neutralized and I would never be able to be used by God again for anything of consequence.

I'm here to announce to you, not only are those things not true, but I feel younger and stronger each day. All my regular checkups since that time have been better than good. Once you recognize the enemy's voice, you will never again believe his lies. My doctor, a marathon runner, recently expressed that he was jealous of my blood

Rescued

pressure and cholesterol counts. All my blood work is great. This is the miracle of God's healing power that I know and love. I want everyone who hears my story to be encouraged and strengthened in their own difficult or seemingly hopeless situation. God is good!

My life is completely different. I am not primarily concerned about what others may think of the things I went through. Rather, I am interested in helping and inspiring people to regain their trust in the healing, delivering power of God. Jesus delivered and set me free. I am going to live the rest of my days making the devil pay for what he did to me by helping others recognize the tactics he uses to destroy their lives and keep them in bondage.

Taking Your Life Back

Chapter Twelve

The Warning

In my early days of ministry, I was somewhat proud to say that I was a "take charge, get it done" kind of person. Now I see that the whole "driven" mentality is a subtle trap, a recipe for disaster. How many more ministers, corporate leaders, career people, caregivers, and stay-at-home moms have to crash and burn, ending up in disaster, before we pause long enough to take a good look at ourselves to see what is really going on?

What is the point of doing great things and achieving success in business or ministry, only to lose everything and die prematurely? *It makes no sense.* But until I became one of "them," I didn't understand how important it is to live a balanced life. Are you running on all cylinders in one or two areas of your life, but neglecting other areas…perhaps, the most important areas of your life? I did this for years. I learned the hard way. You don't have to.

God's healing came with some strict instructions and a stern warning. I will never be able to conduct my life the way I did in my younger years. I heard in my heart, "You are to stay in your 'sweet spot' (within the very specific gifts you have been given as a leader and mentor) and the moment you step out of that place, My healing grace will begin to lift off of your life so you will realize what you are doing to your body." This is the wonderful love of God in action. His instructions were a promise, not a threat. You see, God knows *me.* He knows my weaknesses. He understands my tendency to overwork without regard for my health, without me even being aware I'm doing it.

After repenting for basically running my body completely into the ground, I asked God to help me never repeat that cycle again. He graciously answered that request in a way I will have no difficulty recognizing. Although daily I enjoy wonderful strength and vitality, my energy vanishes when I do too much or get involved in things I shouldn't. Many of the things I was responsible for doing in my early years of ministry, I am no longer allowed to do. In fact, in prayer one day, the Lord said, "In the early days you were a builder. From now on, you will be a *father* of builders!" In keeping with that mandate, I want to help you as a father would his son or daughter who doesn't know how to escape the trouble they are in.

I sincerely desire that my story will become a firmly marked path of easy-to-read signs that will help you quickly identify the danger you may be in or the danger you may soon be facing if you continue to ignore the laws the Creator has established for your body. I hope you will then also recognize and get on the path to safety so you can avoid an experience like mine altogether.

In the chapters that follow, we will explore principles that lead to overall wholeness. It is my prayer that you will experience God speaking to you about situations in your life or perhaps even have the knowledge to guide someone else through a similar crisis.

Further, it is my heart-felt desire that you will find answers, healing, deliverance and the freedom I now enjoy, every day of your life.

Taking Your Life Back

Chapter Thirteen

The Caregiver

I have only briefly referred to how difficult this was on my wife during this time. I think now is a great place for her to tell about this season of our life from her perspective. Oftentimes, people fail to realize the emotional strain and physical toll that being the caregiver of someone with a chronic illness can take, so I have asked Donna to share her story here.

The story of how God brought Rick into my heart and life is a romance novel in itself! I will just say that in my young, romantic, teenage prayers, I asked God for a few things that were important to me in a man. My first request was that the man God brought into my life would be strong, yet gentle. I didn't want a weak, wishy-washy man who couldn't make all the hard decisions that go along with marriage and a family. Secondly, I asked that the man I would marry be serious…as serious as I was about God and all things pertaining to Him. But I didn't want him to be so serious that he couldn't *be* fun or *have* fun. Thirdly, I asked that God would give me someone to protect and love me just as I was, so I could always be myself with him. And oh, just for the asking, I wanted him to be tall, dark and handsome…optional, but "icing on the cake." Well, those prayers were answered beyond all my expectations, and Rick and I have been happily married since we were teenagers. Until illness struck, I had never known Rick as anything but strong, decisive, protective and loving.

Rick has a mischievous sense of humor and a genuine love of fun that he got from his mother. Our marriage has always seemed wonderful to us. He was my loving tower of strength during some dark times I went through due to some childhood hurts. I never, ever dreamed that I would see him as anything but strong.

I began to get a little concerned for the first time when Rick developed a "buzzing in his head," a few years prior to his illness. It was an initial warning sign that neither of us recognized at the time. But when it went away after a short time of sleeping and rest, like Rick, I didn't think any more about it. When his travel schedule got crazy and he couldn't get over jet lag, I thought that sooner or later, the traveling would slow down and it would no longer present a problem. My first realization that we were in for some trouble was when he felt completely exhausted before he had even left home to go on that very important three-week mission trip with Garrett.

Though I excitedly anticipated Rick's return, what I saw when he arrived home *shocked* me! He was very pale, weak, and feverish. I thought it was a relapse of the flu because he was so achy all over. I didn't know then that when skin is painful to the touch, it is often a sign that shingles is alive in the nerves, looking for a weak place to erupt. Now, when others have that symptom, I know that immediate, complete rest is vital to stop the disease in its tracks. I have since found this to be true from my own experience of having shingles twice. To this day, Rick is absolutely adamant if my skin becomes painful to the touch that I stop everything I am involved in and rest completely. From my observation and experience, in most cases, complete rest is the most important action required to remedy the problem.

When Rick broke out in a rash and was in excruciating pain, I was desperate to get him help. I had never seen him in this condition before so I immediately went to all of my reference books to see if I could pinpoint what was going on with him. Through my research, I thought the rash was possibly shingles, but because it was in an unusual place at the base of his spine, I did not know if that was a correct assumption.

All the drama with the first doctor we went to caused me to alternate between being furious and feeling utterly helpless. Though our first line of defense was typically prayer and speaking healing scriptures, I was also determined to do everything I could in the natural realm. I researched and studied nutrition and supplements to find anything that would counteract the symptoms Rick was experiencing.

Soon after the diagnosis, I discovered that the 29 hours Rick spent sitting on the plane in addition to his immune system being compromised by the flu allowed the herpes virus (shingles) to track from his spinal fluid to the weakened nerves at the base of his spine. The first months of his illness were stressful but I thought surely it would not last long. Prayer, faith and speaking God's Word had brought us through every other situation we had faced, so I assumed this would be no different. As the months wore on, Rick's condition did not improve but actually began to worsen.

In fact, most of the time, Rick was in such a state that he could hardly stand for me to be out of his sight. Yet, both of us knew that I had to take on some of the responsibilities that he could no longer handle. It was extremely difficult to leave him. All the time I was dealing with church and school issues, a part of me was continually concerned and thinking about Rick. My life revolved completely around doing anything and everything possible to care for and protect him. I made myself his buffer. I filtered all the information he needed to be told so that it wouldn't be said in such a way that would upset him. I was in a continual state of watchfulness.

I watched Rick's every expression, especially when he was preaching or in a conversation. I became very adept at being able to perceive instantly when he was losing a word or his train of thought. I tried to stay a little ahead of him once I knew what he was talking about so I could be ready to say the word or a phrase to remind him of what he had been saying. It would make me nervous when I knew he was in a situation in which I wasn't with him, especially towards the end of the ordeal when he was really, really bad. He wasn't capable of handling any kind of stress at that time. For a couple of weeks, I really thought I was going to lose him. I knew if something didn't change soon, he would die.

The light had gone out of his eyes and all I saw was utter despair and hopelessness. He kept praying though. He spent hours before God, pleading for direction, surrendering to His will, and worshiping. I am convinced those times spent with God kept him from giving up completely.

In the years before Rick got sick, he was so playful. We had enjoyed many years of great fun together. I was the only girl in a household of all boys and I learned quickly how not to let them get the better of me. They all knew the one thing that would turn me into a fierce fighter was pinning me down. I hated to be pinned down in any way and rendered helpless. When they would try to restrain me, laughing all the while, their "little mama" would turn into a totally different person, usually able to find a method of counter attack that would force them to release their hold on me.

That was the way I felt much of the time during Rick's long struggle… pinned down by forces I couldn't see. But the fighter welled up within me and gave me strength to press back in the fight for my husband's life. I had my own bad days though. One day I waited until Rick and the boys left the house for some rare time alone. I cried my eyes out in the shower. I banged my head on the wall in frustration while crying out to God for help. Sometimes I felt I would implode because of trying so hard to hold it all together.

Though I am a person who loves people and being around people, in order to recharge, I need solitude. I *need* to be by myself. Looking at beautiful things in nature, conversing with God about them and taking pictures of His handiwork feeds my soul. I love to write. Most of the time I will 'see' something. It is like a living picture of revelation and I used to pray and pray for the ability to paint what I would see.

Many years prior to Rick's illness, I had seen something in prayer and again asked the Lord to give me the ability to paint it. I immediately heard these words distinctly in my heart, "Oh, to paint a picture clear of the Lord I love and hold so dear…" I grabbed my ever-present pen and notebook to write that sentence down. The words kept flowing and I kept writing and this is what was said. "Oh, to paint a picture clear of the One I love and hold so dear, Not with canvas, brush and oil, but with words and phrases I will toil. With loving strokes each phrase I'll turn, for in my heart a picture burns. And I must paint for all to see, the heart of God revealed to me."

Then the Lord spoke clearly to my heart, "Donna, if you paint with canvas, brush and oil, they will only see what *you* see. If you paint with words, then I will paint on the canvas of their heart the picture *I* want them to see."

During all the long years of illness, there were moments when I had quiet times alone with the Lord and He would be so close to me that I could almost tangibly feel His presence. He would talk to me and I would pour out my heart to Him and then He would bless me with a picture and the joy of it would flow out in words. Other times, words on a page were the only release for the pressure that was built up inside me. This was God's incredible grace to me during this time.

Many times I would feel like I was at the end of my rope

because I was denied this solitude. It is out of this solitude that my creativity, especially the prophetic poetry, flowed. I tried so hard to hold it all together for Rick's sake that I felt I would implode. I never wanted to be an added worry for Rick so I tried, sometimes unsuccessfully, to keep him from knowing just how deeply this was affecting me. In my heart I knew that because we were one flesh, one heart so in love for all these years, that we could sense what the other was feeling, though no words were spoken to describe it. This is a priceless treasure that only develops by commitment to love and to endure anything together. Most couples 'leave the mine, just before reaching the gold.' It was kind of funny (though not really) how we would try to protect each other.

Rick rarely told me how bad he really felt, but he didn't have to—I could sense it. I could see it in his eyes…in the way he would get really still when the attacks were bad. I knew he was exerting all his strength to deal with the panic that even the strongest medicines had been unable to stop. Sometimes I just held him without speaking, though I longed to scream at the top of my lungs for this to just go away.

Just before Rick received his healing, the pressure of so many things coming at us at once was crushing us both. I didn't think either one of us would survive one particular day, but somehow God gave us His strength and the will to go on though we both momentarily considered throwing in the towel. I have lived through many difficult things in my life, but never until then was I ever that close to just quitting.

We both tried to behave in such a way that people would not become insecure and frightened because of Rick's condition. *There is a price associated with true leadership.* We were never dishonest about what we were going through, but we chose our words thoughtfully. It is just human nature for people to be free with their opinions about everything and to even speak as if they have first-hand knowledge of the situation when, in truth, they have no idea what is really going on. Knowing this, we made a choice early on to be very discriminating about the number of people we wanted to know about the severity of what we were walking through. Because Rick was and is well known, we knew that telling even a few people about the severity of the situation could lead to exaggerated rumors going everywhere.

We needed *faith* in our corner...not *gossip* and *negativity*. I learned something going through this that I had never fully realized before. That is, even if you try to describe what you are going through to your very best friends, though they love you, they have no way of sympathizing with understanding something they have never personally experienced.

On the other hand, there is an instant bond between people who have shared a similar experience, having dealt with the same emotions, frustration and pain that simply is not present with those who have not. I had never been responsible for the care of someone who was experiencing an ongoing, lengthy illness of this magnitude. Now, I understand *completely* what someone in that situation is experiencing. I can see it in their eyes, hear it in their voice, and feel it in the pit of my stomach. There is no need for more. I understand. I sense their desperation.

When Rick became very ill, I was helpless to "fix" him and make it better for him, though I tried everything in the natural to do so. I was his helpmeet, which is the biblical term for wife. I researched endlessly, made him try every natural "remedy" I thought might work, and probably nagged him in ways I shouldn't have, to do things he just couldn't do. It was very frustrating that nothing either of us tried had a lasting effect. I think the hardest things for me to deal with were the feelings of helplessness, frustration, anger and guilt.

The very hardest part was to admit—*I was sometimes angry with Rick for being sick and weak and not getting better.* It was completely irrational, I know, but it was hard for me to see him physically weak. He had always been so very strong and nothing ever kept him down for long. I was just angry—an emotion I was not very familiar with until then. I felt completely helpless and it angered me!

There were things I absolutely had to discuss with Rick concerning church issues that needed a decision. At times, I could see "that look" that told me he wasn't able to deal with the issue, but I was feeling pressure myself and would press him for an answer. What used to come easily from him without a moment's hesitation had become excruciatingly difficult. *Those times were not happy ones…*

When he was really stressed about church issues, Rick would

have even greater difficulty sleeping and only sheer exhaustion would cause him to be able to do so. Because I was so in tune with his needs during the day, I automatically became watchful over his sleep also. I don't actually know when this began, but it was the Holy Spirit who awakened me the first time Rick stopped breathing in his sleep. All of a sudden, I was awake and I knew something was wrong. I began listening for him to take a breath and he didn't. I nudged him ever so gently, as to not awaken him fully because then he would not be able to go back to sleep. That little movement registered somehow in him and he took a deep gasp for air. That was the last sleep I got that night.

After that first time, I trained myself to listen, even while sleeping, for the sounds of a particular kind of exhale. When I heard it, I would become awake enough to begin counting the seconds until he took another breath. If I reached a certain number and he had not taken a breath, I would gently nudge him in a way I knew would stimulate his brain to remember to breathe. If I awakened him doing this, he would not be able to go back to sleep sometimes for the rest of the night. I came to a place where I felt that if I let my guard down for even a moment and fell into a deep, exhausted sleep and was not aware of his breathing, I might possibly wake up in the morning to find that he was gone. This was a nagging fear that never really left my consciousness. My normal night became one of drifting in and out of sleep and listening to his breathing. To this day I still listen sometimes…and am so thankful for normal breathing when he sleeps.

Another difficult issue I had to deal with was guilt. Because the Word of God was firmly hidden in my heart, I knew that guilt and condemnation are tools that the enemy uses against us. He weighs us down with so much guilt and condemnation that our arms become weary with holding the sword of God's Word aggressively against him.

However, knowing his tactics does *not* automatically prevent a person from having to deal with an onslaught of guilt. In my case, I felt guilty that I couldn't come up with an answer to Rick's physical problems. I felt guilty that I couldn't "fix" the situation. I felt really guilty over the anger that I felt and that I would even feel anger at all—no matter the circumstances. I felt guilty that I would get frustrated. *I even felt guilty for feeling guilty!* After all, I wasn't the one who was battling for my life.

I became tired—really, really tired. But God would send someone at those moments to cover me in prayer with encouragement and love. It was like balm to my weary soul…an infusion of strength and courage to stand again, unafraid, with my face to the howling wind of the battle. I am thankful and so grateful for God's wonderful grace! I know many people whose story didn't turn out so well, and I hurt for them. But God is faithful, and I know that without a doubt. He can be trusted to bring a person through what they thought they could never survive.

I asked Rick in our very darkest moment when our hearts were crushed, if a person could die from grief. He couldn't even answer because he was feeling the same deep grief I was feeling. I can tell you honestly, you may think you are going to die and that your life is over, but God is greater than even that. He will bring you through—He did Rick and me.

As Rick often says, "Every day is a precious gift. Live it with thankfulness, even in your darkest moments. God's love will be the light that guides you through to a better place."

Part 2

Taking Your Life Back

Chapter Fourteen

Natural Laws

There are several natural laws that are vital to maintaining life and health. For example:

· You must eat the right foods

· You must get the right amount of sleep

· You must have down time, a Sabbath, when you really stop and rest both your mind and body

We are not machines that are designed to be "on" all the time. All of these simple concepts are as important as working. Without these principles, we won't be able to work forever and our bodies won't be able to fight exhaustion and disease.

In the life of Elijah, it was interesting that when he was discouraged and depressed, God fed him a good meal and gave him rest. This was probably because Elijah wasn't eating right or sleeping properly. He received a miracle, and thank God, miracles still happen today. But generally speaking, God is not going to continually do for you what He requires you to do for yourself.

It *is* possible to slow your pace and produce more. It *is* possible to eat right, exercise, rest adequately and increase your productivity. I did. Today, I am mentally alert, my body is well, and I have strength. I am living a normal life. I woke up this morning full of joy. I kissed my wife and even sang to her before she got out of bed.

Many people spend a lifetime looking for such joy.

People ask me, "Pastor Rick, what happened to you? There is something different about you now." Well, of course, there is something different. *Everything is different!* I feel like the blind man everybody questioned about what had happened to him. He said, "I don't know what happened! All I know is this man Jesus came. I was blind, and now I see" (author's paraphrase of John 9:25).

I am compelled to share these things out of gratitude to the Lord for His healing grace. Also any kind of legitimate healing testimony in which God delivers and heals someone, inspires faith. Good testimonies give others courage during the battles of life. What God has done in my life, He wants to do for you. But in order for Him to help, you need to give heed to natural laws, as well as spiritual laws.

Chapter Fifteen

The Solution

In addition to natural laws, there are spiritual laws. Victory over problems in life—whether physical illness, mental torment, family trouble, financial trouble or any other kind of trouble—depends on an understanding of your personal authority. Many times we are led to believe that the responsibility lies solely with God and is conditional on whether it is "His will" or not to heal or deliver us out of our terrible situation. Jesus stated His position on this very clearly on a number of occasions. On one occasion, He let it be known that it was "the thief," not God, who is out to steal from us, kill us, or to destroy us (John 10:10).

If we really and truly believed the words of Jesus, we wouldn't be so casual about putting up with so much junk. When we allow even a small advancement, the enemy who is out to destroy us will take that as a "go" to bring everything he has in his arsenal against us. I was as guilty of passivity as anyone else, but I learned that lesson the long, hard and painful way. I don't want anyone else to go through what Donna and I went through to learn this truth.

For several decades now, I have been a student of "authority"—the authority of Christ, which He delegated to all who believe in Him. The dictionary defines "authority" as the power to determine or otherwise settle disputes; the right to control, command, or determine. This authority is the power and right that every child of God has been given. We are supposed to exercise authority (the right to control, command, or determine) over demonic powers, illness, lack and everything else that comes to destroy. Jesus died and rose again specifically for the purpose of equipping us to walk through this life the way He did.

Jesus was very clear in His intentions when He called His disciples together and gave them power and authority over all demons. He also gave them authority to cure diseases. Then He sent them out to exercise that power and authority (see Luke 9:1 and Matthew 10:1). When the disciples returned, they were filled with joy (Luke 10:17). Perhaps they weren't expecting the same results that Jesus had experienced, but they discovered that this delegated authority worked through them also. In other words, they found by experience that God had really given them personal authority to help suffering humanity.

This same idea was echoed again when Jesus declared that it was through the revelation of who He is—the Christ, the Savior and Redeemer of all mankind—that He would build His church. The word "church" was never used until this pronouncement. He also firmly declared that His church would be strong enough that the very gates of hell would not overcome it!

He then gave the keys necessary for that to become a reality, the keys of binding and loosing. He declared that if believers would take the authority given to them and bind the enemy from operating in a certain area, then heaven would back the declaration with results. Just think, all of heaven is waiting for us to use our authority.

The same principle applies with the key of loosing. Many times when I pray over a situation or a person, I will bind the enemy's operation in their life and loose the power of God for healing, finances, and deliverance from bondage. This isn't difficult to exercise. We just have to remember who we are in Christ and the authority we have been given through Him (see Matthew 16: 18-19).

For example, it doesn't do any good for a young man to know that he has been given a position of power and responsibility in his father's company if he doesn't choose to acknowledge that fact and walk in it. He may as well be a mail clerk or janitor, because even though both of these positions are valuable in running a company, neither has the authority to make important decisions like the son has been given.

We have been given an awesome privilege as sons and daughters in the Kingdom of God. It is a shame that so few Christians take advantage of this authority. I believe in the days ahead, all of this is going to change. We were made in God's image. He has given us dominion and authority. It is time we act upon these wonderful realities (see Genesis 1:28).

Chapter Sixteen

The Will, Authority and Power

As I said earlier, I realize that because my illness had lasted for such a long time and it had been so long since I felt normal, I had forgotten what normal was like. It is amazing how a person subconsciously adapts in order to cope with what they are going through. I had learned how to adapt but I didn't realize that this adaptation was a crucial factor that was hindering my ability to recover. Adapting in that kind of situation is dangerous because a person begins to lower his expectations to match what he is experiencing. When we settle for so much less than God's best because we are so beaten down by our circumstances, we begin to lose the strength of one of God's greatest gifts to humanity—the will (which is the power to choose one's own actions).

I already knew and understood that the key to man's authority is his will. But in practice, I had let this truth slip. It happened slowly over time, in tiny increments. If it had not occurred so gradually, I would have realized what was happening and would have stopped the decline. When the attacks kept coming and didn't stop, even when I thought I was standing strong against them, their length and intensity wore me down to the point that I eventually caved in under the pressure of it all. I stopped making right choices.

I am reminded of hearing Senator John McCain reflect on his prisoner-of-war days. He said that he was able to remain strong for a long time, but the injuries inflicted continually on his body and mind eventually broke him. I understood his statements all too well. I have seen far too many broken people walking around suffering....existing....surviving—but not really living. I want this unnecessary suffering to stop!

How can a student of authority, who knows and walks in his authority, possibly lose his understanding of what this means? I may have never fully understood the answer to that question without the 6 1/2 year experience I went through. Prior to the awakening I experienced, I didn't have enough knowledge about the importance of my will (my ability to choose my own actions) as it relates directly to my authority (the right to control, command, or determine). I didn't fully understand how vital my will was, much less, that it was the single most important key to me being able to walk in authority as is my right and privilege.

Our will is our "chooser." It's that simple. We make hundreds of choices a day without much thought at all. I didn't realize or appreciate what an amazing gift my will was until I lost the ability to exercise it. When I'm hungry, I choose what I'm going to eat after a few milliseconds of deciding what sounds good to me at the moment, without even thinking about the enormous gift of being able to make this choice.

Choosing paints action pictures. I can choose to walk into my house because I want to. I can walk into my house anytime I want to because it is mine. I don't have to ask for permission. Since the day the owner gave me the keys, I have possessed full authority to do whatever I choose to, in regard to my house. I don't have to call the former owner and wait for him to come and do what he gave me the keys and authority to do as the new owner. Choice is an amazingly precious gift! I will never again take the privilege of choice for granted.

In essence, Jesus said, "When I came to earth, I lived and made choices based on the authority I was given by my Father, Creator of all mankind. I spoke His words. I did His works. I showed you by example and taught you as much as you could possibly understand about how authority works. Then, the time came that My work was done, and I had to leave. So, even as my Father sent me, I send you. With all the same wisdom and power that was available to me through the Holy Spirit, I send you to do the Father's works. I send you to exercise authority for yourself. I know you will make mistakes, but I also know you will learn from those experiences. I have made it clear that you are an overcomer. I have given you a powerful sword, along with the authority and responsibility to swing it! As you grow stronger, more will be required of you. Only by growing, will you be able to experience the victory that I have for you in every area of your life. As you are faithful and exercise My authority in the smallest things, remember that I will make you ruler over all that I have. You will reign with Me for eternity! You can overcome in life because I will always be with you—don't ever forget that."

Here are three things that you must never forget...

• **Your *will* is your chooser and is the key to unlocking your authority.**

You have the awesome and unique ability to choose to let circumstances destroy you, or you can choose to NOT let them destroy you. That is choosing to live by the authority God has given you to overcome.

• **Your *authority* is the door to God's power that your will chooses to unlock in every situation.**

When you make a choice that no matter how difficult the circumstance is, you will not give in, give up, or back down; then you are filled with the same measure of God's strength, energy and power as the determination of your choice.

• ***God's power* is the very realm of victory in your life.**

Strength and energy now fills you because of the choice you have made, which in turn enables you to stand and declare what God says is true in the face of every adverse situation. His power sustains and keeps you focused—not on the circumstances, but on the fact that these circumstances do not rule you or determine your final outcome! When you step into this realm of victory, time is no longer something the enemy can use as a weapon against you. As far as you are concerned, it is done and when that victory manifests in the natural is no longer an issue for you to worry about.

I didn't realize that the only way to access and activate my authority was through my will (my chooser). If I don't *choose* to walk in the authority God has given me, no one else has the right to walk in that authority for me. No one can make me do anything I don't want to do unless at some point, I choose to give into force. If I choose to give in, it is still my choice, whether forced or not. What amazing power! This is why our will is the enemy's number one target. Our will and ability to choose is what he wants most to be under his control.

All the forces of evil know that once a person decides to accept Jesus Christ as Lord and Savior, though they try everything in their power to stop that decision from being made, evil forces are powerless in the face of that choice. They are rendered completely powerless. They cannot prevent the transformation that follows this choice.

Knowledge of the power of our freedom to choose is actually what terrifies the enemy most. All the forces of darkness are bent on neutralizing or controlling that wonderful gift in our lives. Used properly, under the guidance of God's Word, our authority to choose is the one ability that can thwart every evil plan devised to destroy our life of victory. The only access you have to your authority is through your will, which is the seat of government in your life— your ability to choose.

You have become the person you are now because of the choices you have made. In other words, we are free moral agents. We have the ability to choose life or death. God has given us dominion to such a degree that whatever He has given us authority over, He will no longer take authority over for us. We must decide by conscious thought to operate according to the Word, taking our God-given authority and putting it into action in all areas of our life. Knowing and practicing these truths are vital to living successfully while on this earth.

I understood authority so well at one time. So how was the enemy able to get my will neutralized and in his grasp? Little by little, the enemy lulls us into acceptance. The book of Daniel reveals that one of the enemy's main tactics is to wear down the saints in order to get entrance to, and try to take control of this area of our lives above all others. "And he shall speak great words against the most High, and shall wear out the saints of the most High, and think to change times and laws: and they shall be given into his hand until a time and times and the dividing of time" (Daniel 7:25).

Satan has a very elaborate strategy devised against each one of us. He has attacks devised to wear us out and wear us down by difficulties—physical, mental, financial, and relational. By keeping the pressure on in one or more of these areas, a person can become stressed. Unrelenting stress wears a person down mentally and emotionally. At that point, Satan can slowly but surely set up a battlefield of thoughts in your mind. This onslaught is designed to cause you to question yourself and ultimately question God's intentions for your life. Then the enemy will proceed with his intricate plan to breed doubt about everything. This is how he compromises the integrity of your will. This is what happened to me.

Satan knows very well what you need to remember at all times—the only access you have to authority is through your will.

Your authority is your access to victory. Therefore, he attacks you viciously and vigorously to get to your will, in order to disable any authority that you could use to stop him. The enemy's goal is to come in through this particular method so your thinking will become clouded, causing you to slip into passivity. You stop choosing to resist him. Your strength diminishes. You don't make decisions or take risks. You become afraid, passive and weak until you no longer walk in authority.

The only avenue to your authority is through your will. Your will must be kept intact. People say, "Well, I surrender my will to God." No, you don't! God doesn't want your will. He gave you your will. Your will and your ability to choose distinguish you from every other thing God has made. He wants your will submitted to Him through obedience to His Word. He has no use for a surrendered will; He has no interest in controlling your will. Instead, *He wants to help you align your will with His, so you will make the right choices.* Even in this, He actively works with you by giving you the "how to" in His Word. When you obey, the Holy Spirit strengthens you with grace to be able to do what you have *chosen* to do.

Exercising your authority is not really hard or complicated. It simply requires a little more effort than we are sometimes willing to give. Laziness is a choice. God respects your choices so highly that He will not violate them, even the detrimental ones. In reality, our will is the most precious and prized possession God has given us, and we should esteem the power of choice accordingly.

God is not interested in controlling your will, nor is He going to exercise authority over that which you need to take authority over. But the enemy will certainly push, control, and endeavor to take over at every opportunity. God gave you the power of choice so you can choose to walk in the authority that He has given you, in order to deal with the circumstances and situations that confront you.

The whole process I just described is the exact strategy the enemy used to wear down my will. The non-stop pressure and stress of failing health, along with a host of other circumstances I had no control over, had begun to eat away at my ability to choose—my ability to think clearly, to stand, to think cognitively—all of which ultimately compromised my ability to make right choices and take risks.

Chapter Seventeen

Fear

One of the most successful ways the enemy compromises the integrity of our will is by bringing fear into our lives. I am not referring to specific fears such as the fear of flying, fear of crowds, or fear of spiders, although the enemy is the author of all of these fears. Instead, I am referring to a different class of fear. There is a fear the enemy tries to bring against us that is not readily identifiable, but it is a generalized, abiding fear. This kind of fear pervades our culture today; provoked mainly through widespread media and the stress of the times we are living in.

Think about it. Every day we hear about troubles in our world, see horrifying images, and feel emotions about people we don't even know in places we have usually never visited simply by the operation of a remote control, a mouse or a mobile phone. Many people are even addicted to this type of information, feeling they have to know what is going on.

Every loss of life is horrible, and in fact, most of the ways that loss occurs have been going on from the very beginning of humanity. The difference today is that we hear about and see catastrophes, tragedies and loss of life daily as opposed to times past. The world seems to be going the wrong direction. The constant exposure to so much sadness and despair creates a generalized sense of hopelessness. When we fill our minds with reports of atrocities that we have no control over, our sense of God's greatness is diminished. We lose sight of the fact that we are safe in the palm of His hands, as we live and conduct our lives in obedience to Him.

As we become increasingly focused on the sadness in our world, the spirit of fear begins to creep in. The enemy takes advantage of this place that we have opened and comes in with a sense of fear and foreboding that is paralyzing. This is the simple and methodic way in which the enemy routinely discourages us and makes us feel out of control of our own situation.

During this time if you had asked me if I had any fear, I would have said, "Absolutely not." By nature, I have never been a fearful person. I'm normally not afraid of things. So, how then did fear enter in and begin to control my life? I have come to the realization that anxiety is simply fear. Do you know what panic is? Panic is paralyzing, tormenting fear.

Fear compromises your will and ability to choose. Fear brings you to a place where you are afraid of what your choices will cause to happen in your life. I didn't even realize it, but through all that happened to me—one bad thing after another—I became afraid that I wasn't going to have a future. I became afraid that I would never be able to function with strength and confidence as I had before. Somewhere in the back of my head, I was afraid that somehow I was reaping all of this as punishment from God for some unknown, unconfessed wrong. It didn't matter that this was totally against all I knew from many years of Bible study and walking in close fellowship with God.

In my heart, I felt like I had earnestly been doing the best I could to serve Him well. But the enemy kept seeding my soul with nagging doubts and questions: "Is it *me*? Is this *God*? You surely don't want to be rebellious against God's will for your life." If I had not been so stressed and worn out from fighting the other issues, I would have seen these thoughts as lies of the enemy and would have dealt with them accordingly, swiftly and decisively. As it was, I became afraid of so many things. In fact, during that season, other people were unwittingly reinforcing what I was hearing on the inside. The enemy was using well-meaning people to tell me negative things about myself, pointing out that in my weakened state, I was not a good leader anymore. This made me feel like I was not even a good person. I had all kinds of negative things spoken over me as a child in school, and it was hard to hear those types of things again from people I loved. I began to be afraid I could never again measure up to my former standards. That fear fed the anxiety and panic attacks.

Do you know what a panic attack or an anxiety attack is? It is fear of fear itself. It is internalized fear. Let me explain it with this illustration: One day something happens and your heart begins to pound. Often there isn't a reason that stands out to account for the sudden sense of anxiety. The attack seems to come out of nowhere. You hyperventilate, feeling like you are suffocating. You feel closed in and claustrophobic, having an almost irresistible urge to run or get out of where you are. You don't feel safe. The bad part is, when you go somewhere else, you don't feel safe there either. This unsafe feeling follows you, causing you to feel completely vulnerable and out of control in the situation. Your whole body reacts to these feelings.

Imagine suddenly slamming on your car brakes to avoid a terrible accident. A physical rush comes over your whole body, leaving you horribly weak and physically drained. You don't want to ever experience a repeat of those feelings again. The dread of a repeat encounter is exactly the same dread people face with panic attacks. You frantically rack your brain to pinpoint the elusive cause in order to prevent a reoccurrence. Then, you begin to obsess about how awful the anxiety was, and you become increasingly afraid of a repeat experience. You become preoccupied with the possibility that at any moment, you will find yourself out of control again, desperately hoping that you won't. If and when another attack occurs, the feelings are compounded because now, what you were afraid was going to happen, does.

At least in my experience, the compounded fear caused the attacks to grow exponentially worse. Each additional attack seemed worse than the one before. Without even realizing it, I became preoccupied with fear and dread. I always felt that if only I could be prepared, the attacks wouldn't be so severe, but they always came in moments when I was not anticipating them. The inability to predict the attacks in and of itself added yet another layer of fear. I felt as if some unseen assailant, always close and ready to pounce, was mercilessly stalking me. I became very afraid of being afraid—and didn't even realize what was happening. The cycle was subtle and well camouflaged behind the actual attacks. That's what panic is—fear of fear itself.

This new understanding helped me immensely. The knowledge empowered me and provided me with something concrete that I could deal with. I learned how to face fear, calling it what it was. Anxiety and panic can be very general and hard to identify. Fear, on the other hand, is easy to see. When I realized that panic and anxiety were simply the same as fear...*the game was over.*

You can become worn down through this kind of torment and fear, to the point of feeling that it is useless to try to fight anymore. This is when passivity begins to set in. Passivity is a false, unproductive coping mechanism that activates particularly in situations that are long and drawn out. Passivity occurs when you decline into a state of giving in or giving up. There is actually a spirit of passivity that can invade one's life. I am going to tell you the process of how that happens and how the spirit of passivity works, so you can recognize and deal with it properly in your own life.

Taking Your Life Back

Chapter Eighteen

Passivity

In order to understand passivity, there must first be a clear understanding of how God operates in our lives and how the enemy attempts to thwart His work. God draws us to Himself. He speaks to us and invites us into a relationship with Him through Jesus. After we accept Jesus as our Savior and ask Him to forgive and cleanse us of our sins, we become part of the family of God. As we talk to Him in prayer and read His Word, we see the ways we need to change. Then the Holy Spirit helps us to make those changes.

God never does our part for us or against our will. He never forces us to obey any of the principles laid out plainly in His Word to help us become a better person. He will not control us. He is love. God waits for us to receive His invitation to become all that He has made us to be through the birth, death and resurrection of His Son. The Holy Spirit invites and encourages us through the Word of God to become all we are destined to be. He is a gentleman and waits on our choice to proceed with His strength.

The enemy, on the other hand, operates very differently. He doesn't invite. That is totally against his nature. He manipulates in order to bring circumstances to a point where they seem to be beyond our control. His aim is to take our focus off of God so that we will not speak His promises over that area of concern. With our focus diverted, the enemy then insidiously, maliciously begins his campaign to gain control through fear.

Control is the whole focus of the enemy's plan. He will use every tool in his inventory to establish control of any targeted area of your life. He never stands in front of you, waving his arms so you can easily recognize his strategy. Instead, he subtly whispers into your thoughts. When his suggestions are entertained, he quickly builds a center of strength in that particular thought pattern from which he will endeavor to build further influence in other areas of your thinking.

When you are in control of your will, anytime you say "no" with conviction, the devil has absolutely no power whatsoever to continue. Your authoritative stance renders him helpless. When you decide to accept Jesus as your Lord and Savior, he will try to feed you reasons why that isn't a good idea. When you choose to ignore those thoughts, all hell can't stop your decision. That is the amazing power our God has given uniquely to human beings.

The enemy's game is simply *control*. There has been a subtle lie successfully perpetrated throughout the Christian culture that has allowed the enemy almost unlimited access into the lives of God's people. It is the lie that being strong-willed isn't a good or virtuous trait. People often confuse strong-willed with self-willed. We are not talking about rebellion against God by doing something "my way," instead of the way that is plainly laid out for us in the Bible.

Being strong-willed, within the parameters that God has given, is one of your greatest gifts from Him. Your will should be very strong to please the God who created and loves you. That means we should all live our lives in a very purposeful way, looking at the Word, considering our lives, and making decisions to live accordingly.

In over thirty years of experience in pastoring people, many have said to me, "I don't have any control over this particular sin." To suggest that a Christian has no control over temptation is a lie. However, each time you open the door to sin in your life, you are surrendering the strength of your will to the enemy. At any such opportunity, the enemy immediately advances in an endeavor to control you in a greater way. *He is methodically plotting a hostile takeover.* His invitation for you to return to that sin gains momentum. That is why the desire and temptation grows much stronger after being yielded to. Each time you choose to give in, that sin has been given permission to dig in and latch on to establish a greater hold. By choosing to give in to that temptation, you have submitted your authority to it and are now in subjection to it. You have become a slave by your own choice.

This same principle works in exactly the same way when we choose to not give in. Every choice to not give in, establishes more strength to make the same right choice when confronted again. So, the principle works both ways. One choice makes us weaker, while the other makes us stronger. The enemy attempts to compromise our will so that he can bring us to a state of passivity. He cannot control us, unless we stop controlling ourselves. He cannot control me if I'm still controlling my own destiny with the power of God in my life. He will do anything to bring us to a place of neutrality—a place of surrender.

There is a strong scriptural principle of waiting upon the Lord. In other words, when I pray every morning, I sit in His presence. I bask in His love. I talk to Him. I love Him with my words, and I feel His love washing over me. This is waiting upon the Lord (see Isaiah 40:31). Waiting on the Lord is always an activity. I am an active participant in this meditation. My mind is being filled with His Word and His thoughts. I am fully engaged with my will moving toward God.

This kind of meditation and waiting on the Lord is not a state of neutrality where we step into a state of nothingness, abandoning any kind of thought, waiting for God to fill the void and the emptiness. This is where a lot of good people who really love God get into trouble. Neutrality instantly opens the door to the enemy and is always the first requirement for anyone in the occult to access the demonic realm. In our life, Christian meditation should be centered on the Word of God and fellowshipping with the Lord with active participation of our heart and thoughts.

There are three major ways in which the enemy works to bring you to a point of spiritual passivity:

1. Wrong Thinking

As fear began to come in and my situation began to grow worse over time, I became overwhelmed. In my heart, I thought I was doing everything I knew to do according to the Scriptures to get better. When nothing seemed to be changing, thoughts bombarded my mind. I didn't recognize them for what they were—subtle questions, laced with doubt, which slowly but steadily inched me away from continuing to stand in authority against the unrelenting physical attacks.

Seemingly innocent statements came to mind such as: "Rick, you know the problem isn't with God or His Word, so the problem has to be with you." When I entertained these thoughts, my confidence began to diminish. Though it is true that the problem is never on God's end, I didn't even stop to consider the real source—the real enemy. I asked myself questions like, "What am I doing wrong? What am I not doing right?" In this particular case, the Holy Spirit didn't indicate to me that I was doing anything wrong or failing to do what was right. Subtly, my focus was drawn away from confidence in God's Word to questioning, second-guessing, and doubting myself. That shift in my thinking led me to feel that it was somehow up to me to make this all change. I became dull to what had always been a sharp reality in my mind and heart before—it's all because of God's grace. Nothing is contingent on my efforts apart from grace. That course of wrong thinking led me to a place of hopelessness. I was doing everything I could…right? I was doing the best I could…right? My best obviously wasn't good enough then, was it? I had to do something. I had to do something more.

The only other thing I knew to do was to worship, so I threw myself into worship, thinking that my worship would do it. Worship is beautiful—right? Of course it is. But I had changed the motive of my worship and that was wrong. This seems so obvious to me now that I wonder why I didn't see it then. What a wonderful joy it is to be brought to a place to clearly recognize such a diabolical trap and to be able to expose it for what it is. My worship became such that I would cry tears of devotion and say, "God, if nothing ever changes, I will still worship You. I live to worship You," and I really meant it. It sounded so noble and self-sacrificing, yet within that statement was a subtle questioning of His character, integrity and faithfulness to His Word. I no longer spoke His Word of healing over my life with authority—I was "surrendered" to His will. He had never told me in His Word that He wanted me to live this way for the rest of my life. Deep in my heart, I knew He didn't really want that for me. I had fallen into the trap of changing my theology to accommodate my circumstances.

This seemingly spiritual attitude was a disguise for passivity and false surrender. Over the long years of sickness, the enemy painstakingly infiltrated this attitude into my mind. I need to clarify the deception in my surrender so you will be able to recognize false surrender in your own situations. In reality, I have always been surrendered to God in the fact that I have always been committed to obey Him and His Word. That decision is a choice of my will that is foundational. The false surrender was not to God, but rather to the circumstances. This type of surrender is completely against God's Word and against everything Jesus died to attain for me. My surrender at this time was a choice to quit fighting and standing for my healing. I did this under the ugly religious white flag of "If it is Your will." I was choosing to not exercise my will to fight and live. I was right where the enemy wanted me, and nearly lost my life because of it.

In my surrender, I allowed whatever to happen without resisting or even lifting my voice, just in case the circumstance was actually God's will. I thought I was pleasing God in my situation by saying, "If nothing ever changes, I live to worship You." (This type of thinking was completely opposite of everything I had ever believed or taught.) I can't believe how absurd my thinking became. I'm so thankful that the Lord revealed to me the error of my thinking. It suddenly dawned on me that in adapting an attitude of surrender to circumstances of any kind that are opposite of what God says He wants for me, I was unwittingly denying the very reason Jesus came to earth. In this twisted way of thinking, my new theology placed our dear Lord Jesus in partnership with panic attacks, anxiety, fear, depression and discouragement. This kind of thinking is completely opposite of reality. This kind of religious thinking will steal a person's very life.

"The thief cometh not, but for to steal, and to kill, and to destroy: I am come that they might have life, and that they might have it more abundantly" (John 10:10). What are you going to do with these gracious words that fell from the lips of the Master? "I am come that they might have life…" What I was suffering through was anything but the abundant life. "Peace I leave with you, my peace I give unto you; not as the world gives, give I unto you. Let not your heart be troubled, neither let it be afraid" (John 14:27).

Jesus promised peace, but I had no peace whatsoever. "Fear not, little flock; for it is your Father's good pleasure to give you the kingdom" (Luke 12:32).

Jesus instructed us on more than one occasion to not be afraid, but I was living in constant fear. Something was very wrong with that picture. Do you think that being tormented and terrorized is the will of God? What in the world did Jesus come to deliver us from anyway? Someone may answer, "Well, it was to save us from our sins." Yes, but the implications of being saved from our sins are so much more. There was no fear or lack in the Garden of Eden before sin entered. There was no depression or anxiety. Sin gave birth to all of these negative forces. Jesus came to redeem the whole man....spirit, soul and body.

2. Wrong Believing

Through the long years of battling sleeplessness, anxiety and loss of confidence, I began to change how I looked at my situation. Though I had once been rooted and grounded in the Word of God, I began to change my beliefs according to what I was experiencing. It was the only way to live without struggling. Stupidly, I began to think seemingly spiritual thoughts like, Well, Rick, maybe you will give glory to God through people watching you stay so pure and strong in the midst of all these years of this junk happening in your life. It never ceases to amaze me how we can manufacture all kinds of crazy excuses when we decide that we don't want to fight anymore because the fight is too hard. Though I understand those feelings from my own experience, the alternative to fighting is costly beyond words. Many times what actually happens during an extended trial, after years of suffering, we gradually change our theology—our belief system—to accommodate our experience. Wrong thinking leads to wrong believing. Both of these things open the doorway to the enemy.

3. Wrong Praying

I gradually quit praying prayers of authority and replaced them with prayers of weakness. I got to the point where I was so worn down that I started praying, "God, if it is Your will that I deal with this the rest of my life to somehow bring You glory, then Lord, I want You to know I am going to serve You, and I'm going to love You regardless." The moment I began to accept that I would live in a weakened state for the rest of my life, I began thinking that somehow God was going to use all of this junk to bring Himself glory. I entered into passivity. In lowering my will, I gave up my authority and faith, replacing it with a flag of surrender to the enemy.

After reading the chapter on passivity in the book I mentioned earlier, the whole remaining part of that day I prayed, "God, please show me what to do," and I began to repent. One of the first things I repented of was praying those passive prayers like, "God, if nothing ever changes, if it's just Your will the rest of my life for me to be this way, I am going to glorify You." Those types of prayers seem so spiritual…but they are wrong and can be fatal.

The enemy was running roughshod over my life, and I was

somehow beginning to partially attribute all this to God. I wasn't accusing God directly. But in saying, "Well, if it is Your will," I was in effect making Him a partner to the work of the enemy. When you develop that kind of mentality, it literally prevents you from ever getting rid of the problem because you short-circuit your authority. The enemy has securely captured your will, thereby also binding your ability to take authority.

This revelation came to me on January 15, 2006. For the next several days, I prayed and repented over many things. As a matter of fact, God started revealing things to me at an amazing rate. The Lord showed me clearly three specific entry points that the enemy had used to gain that level of stronghold in my life.

1) Sin

There were sins in my life that the Lord had me repent of such as the drivenness that got me into this in the first place, as well as putting ministry above common sense and well-being. When the doctor said I had to leave my ministry responsibilities for a time in order to recover and I said that I couldn't, this meant that I was carrying a greater load of responsibility than had actually been placed on me. I was receiving a good deal of self-worth from what I was doing and had forgotten that all my worth has to come from who I am in Christ alone. I had to repent of all this. Yes, pastors have sins, and they need to admit them and deal with them. Sins that seem justifiable yet are breaking God's laws must be recognized for what they are and repented of.

2) Breaking Natural Laws

Many times we break natural laws. Here is a list of some common natural laws.

· Not getting proper rest

· Overworking

· Abusing your schedule

· Abusing your body

· Abusing your mind

You were not designed to be engaged all the time. God created a Sabbath. You are the temple of the Holy Spirit. Care for His temple!

3) Permitting Fear

Ultimately, I allowed fear to enter and control my life by not controlling my thoughts. I knew better. I worked through all these issues and repented. Now, I wake up every morning and thank God that I am free. I thank Him that I am delivered from fear. I thank God that He broke the powers of sin off of my life. I thank God that He has delivered me from prescription drugs. I thank God that He has healed my body from immune system breakdown and adrenal failure. People wonder why I am so excited when I speak. I have my life back! I can hardly contain the joy that each new day brings. It's a wonderful life.

This can be a healing moment for you. God healed me, and He wants to heal you too. God delivered me, and He will do the same for you. God wants to deliver you from fear, depression, panic attacks, and mental torment of any kind. He will do it for you. If you have sickness in your body or disease of any kind, He wants to heal you. Jesus is a Healing Jesus.

Begin now to praise God aggressively with thanksgiving. Step out in faith—go beyond your comfort zone and fill your mouth with praise, thanking Him for making a way for you to be free from this point forward. As you do this, you will receive your freedom through the healing power of Jesus. The way to defeat the enemy is to exalt the truth of God over the lies the enemy has been feeding you. You cannot stop a negative thought with a negative thought. You must stop a negative thought with a declaration of God's truth spoken out loud. This is a time-tested, scientifically proven principle. - you believe what you hear yourself say more readily than what you hear others say.

You must understand the power contained in the name of Jesus. Everything that Jesus ever did in his earthly ministry and all of God's power and grace are literally released through the Name of Jesus. God has given you that Name to use.

So, when you pray in the Name of Jesus, you are releasing every bit of His power over your specific situation. It is up to you to call on the Name of Jesus. Be assured, He will hear and answer. It is never God's will for anyone He has created to live a life trapped in fear, bondage or sin. This is stated plainly in Scripture so there would be no misunderstanding on this point.

"For this purpose the Son of God was manifested, that He might destroy the works of the devil" (I John 3:8). Ultimately, once you have received your freedom, your participation to maintain freedom will be required. You must be ruthless as I have learned to be, with negativity of all kinds that will seek to entrap and enslave you once again. Making this principle a part of who you are is as vital as gaining your freedom in the first place. You will have to make a choice to control what information you allow to enter into your mind. Pay attention. Think about what you are thinking about!

One of the things I practice, without fail, is that I do not listen to, watch, read or entertain anything negative in the evening before I sleep. It would be so helpful if you would make a choice to do this as well. Though unavoidable issues may arise, you can reduce their effect on you by also practicing, as I do, Philippians 4:6-8, "Be anxious for nothing, but in everything by prayer and supplication, with thanksgiving, let your requests be made known to God; and the peace of God, which surpasses all understanding, will guard your hearts and minds through Christ Jesus. Finally, brethren, whatever things are true, whatever things are noble, whatever things are just, whatever things are pure, whatever things are lovely, whatever things are of good report, if there is any virtue and if there is anything praiseworthy—meditate on these things."

Meditation is simply choosing your thoughts and then thinking on them. You create the very atmosphere of your life by the thoughts you choose. This is what I do on a daily basis. I choose to be happy.

I choose to be thankful. I choose to enjoy every day of my life. Make a choice today to live the good life God has created for you. Do what needs to be done and from this moment forward, begin Taking Your Life Back!

Passivity

The Harrison House Vision

Proclaiming the truth and the power

Of the Gospel of Jesus Christ

With excellence;

Challenging Christians to

Live victoriously,

Grow spiritually,

Know God intimately.

PRAYER OF SALVATION

God loves you—no matter who you are, no matter what your past. God loves you so much that He gave His one and only begotten Son for you. The Bible tells us that "...whoever believes in Him shall not perish but have eternal life" (John 3:16 NIV). Jesus laid down His life and rose again so that we could spend eternity with Him in heaven and experience His absolute best on earth. If you would like to receive Jesus into your life, say the following prayer out loud and mean it from your heart.

Heavenly Father, I come to You admitting that I am a sinner. Right now, I choose to turn away from sin, and I ask You to cleanse me of all unrighteousness. I believe that Your Son, Jesus, died on the cross to take away my sins. I also believe that He rose again from the dead so that I might be forgiven of my sins and made righteous through faith in Him. I call upon the name of Jesus Christ to be the Savior and Lord of my life. Jesus, I choose to follow You and ask that You fill me with the power of the Holy Spirit. I declare that right now I am a child of God. I am free from sin and full of the righteousness of God. I am saved in Jesus' name. Amen.

If you prayed this prayer to receive Jesus Christ as your Savior for the first time, please contact us on the Web at **www.harrisonhouse.com** to receive a free book.

Or you may write to us at
Harrison House • P.O. Box 35035 • Tulsa, Oklahoma 74153

A note from the author...

As a young pastor, just out of Bible College and full of faith, nothing seemed impossible to me in June of 1980. No challenge was too great to tackle in coming back to St. Louis to begin a church with absolutely nothing I could count on except my wife, two boys, fifty dollars, five radio advertisements already produced and a vision as big as the world. I was on fire!

In March of the previous year, I was at a conference in Dallas, Texas. My heart was so hungry for God. I absorbed the messages from every service and couldn't get enough. On the third night, I was lying in bed worshipping God and all of a sudden He gave me a vision. I had never had anything like that happen to me before and only twice since. I wasn't asleep, so it wasn't a dream, but more like watching something on a screen at a theater. I saw people, thousands of them as far as the eye could see. There were two aisles, and wheelchairs lined the one on the right while the one on the left was filled with stretchers.

All the people were sitting with Bibles, pen and paper, listening to me speak and taking notes. Then, all at once the people got up out of their chairs and went to those in the wheelchairs and on the stretchers. As they prayed, the people began to get out of the wheelchairs and off of the stretchers, healed.

I asked God what this was and He replied, "This is a church, My church, and I want you to start it. If you will be faithful and obedient, all you see will come to pass."

"Where?" I asked. "St. Louis," was the immediate reply.

I was so excited I could hardly stand it! Donna was sleeping soundly beside me and I wanted to wake her up to tell her but she was three months pregnant with our second child and I knew she needed to sleep. She was barely awake the next morning when I told her.

We went back to our little church in Bennettsville, South Carolina, resigned and prepared to move so I could go to Bible College for a year in preparation of obeying the vision God had given me. It was like fire inside and I was filled with passion for St. Louis and the people God was giving me to pastor, though I hadn't yet seen one of them.

Through a set of miraculous circumstances and Divine interventions, I wound up at the Bible College God *wanted* me to attend instead of the one I *assumed* He wanted me to attend. This was my first lesson in the fact that 'assumption is the lowest form of knowledge.'

I had just graduated, and through another set of circumstances that challenged my faith, I drove straight to St. Louis, determined to start the church as God ordained and to see the vision come to pass in the first couple of years. (I had not yet fully learned through painful experience that "the trial of your faith works patience –

which has not been one of my greatest virtues.)

With my faith, I was prepared to see and preach to the little hotel conference room packed to capacity (seventy five at the most). Nineteen people showed up – four being me, Donna and our two boys; my Mom and Dad, other family and friends and five new people from the radio spots we had run – one a day for five days – using the fifty dollars I came home with to pay for them.

It didn't matter, every single person was seed for the thousands I saw continually in that vision.

The early years were filled with milestones, miracles, and growth. Everything God spoke to me to do, I did, no matter how impossible it seemed or how "out of the box" it looked. God said that if I would be faithful *and* obedient, all that I saw would come to pass and I was determined that I would be both to the best of my ability.

I had developed a passion for prayer and fellowship with God as well as intense study of His Word when I was still very young in ministry and they remain my greatest passions to this day. I must say, though, even though I am not at all proud of the fact, there were a couple of times in the busyness of administrating the rapid early growth, I slipped into a very dangerous place of riding the wave of successes that were coming instead of prayerfully navigating my heart through them.

I have since seen what I thought to be veterans in Christ crash and burn in the rapids growth and success, so I look back with much thankfulness that God in His mercy yanked me off my high horse privately and gave me a chance to repent of thinking this had anything to do with me at all instead of His grace.

We continued to grow in every way and were favored with God's blessings and continued to move and expand on every side. We had a daily television program, I had a daily radio program that had a very large faithful following for over 20 years. God blessed me with the opportunity to provide a place for ministers to be raised up and sent out to do amazing things – far beyond what God had called me to do. I was never jealous of their success – except once, when the head of our church resource center kept giving me monthly updates of the amount of tapes sales between me and Joyce Meyer, who was a part of my staff and who had a large women's ministry she taught on Thursday mornings. The day he came in and reported she was now selling more of her teaching tapes than I was, I went to the auditorium to talk to God about it.

"I am the senior pastor, Lord. Shouldn't I be selling more tapes than Joyce?" I asked. The Lord gently spoke something to my heart that changed me forever. He said, "Rick, I never called you to be the best preacher, I called you to be the best pastor."

From that moment on, I knew it was all okay and it has been a great joy to see all she and others have gone on to do for Him. I know I am doing the very best I can at what He called *me* to do.

That has been years ago and in the years since I have pastored my church and traveled the nations with another mandate, to mentor and be a strength and encouragement to other pastors, missionaries and leaders as well as to carry the particular message God has given me for them representing Life Christian Church.

We have had some pretty big obstacles to navigate though the years, especially in the 80's when moral failures rocked the whole evangelical church world. But, we came through it stronger. Still, there was nothing in any way so big, intense or long in duration that I and my beloved congregation was challenged to the very core as what I am going to tell you about now.

Everything I had ever known or believed was soon to be tested to its breaking point. I feel, on one hand that the enemy used my own willful ignorance and disobedience concerning taking care of my body as an opportunity to step in and kill me or at the very least to marginalize me so that I would never be able to fulfill the vision God had given me.

I also know that God never wastes an opportunity to prove His greatness and unconditional love for us. In those same trials, meant by the evil one to destroy, God will take those same circumstances and use them as an opportunity to form greater humility and strength of character in those who have a teachable heart. I learned things I could never have possibly learned another way. I experienced a depth in God not found except through the crucible of great pain and suffering and leaning entirely on His grace in order to survive from one moment to the next. There also comes a humility toward others through being able to know from personal experience their suffering that can't be explained in words.

Mostly, when we acknowledge and repent of our own weakness, and failure to obey God's instructions that were meant for our good, He comes quickly, with healing in his wings and restoration in His hand.

This is my heart and prayer for you.

Rick

About the author

Rick Shelton has been the senior pastor of LIFECHURCH in St. Louis, Missouri, for more than 30 years. Beginning with nineteen people and growing to a vibrant congregation of over four thousand members.

Pastor Rick is known for being a very passionate speaker—one who always contends for the power and presence of the Holy Spirit. He has traveled to 30 nations speaking at churches and leadership conferences.

Pastors Rick and Donna live in St. Louis, Missouri where they have raised four sons and are now enjoying their five wonderful grandchildren.